Just Call Me Mom!

Just CALL ME *Mom!*

Mary Tatem

CHRISTIAN PUBLICATIONS
CAMP HILL, PENNSYLVANIA

Christian Publications
3825 Hartzdale Drive, Camp Hill, PA 17011

ISBN: 0-87509-551-8
LOC Catalog Card Number: 94-70693
© 1994 by Mary Tatem
All rights reserved
Printed in the United States of America

94 95 96 97 98   5 4 3 2 1

Cover Design by Linda G. Wood

Dedication

To my three wonderful daughters-in-law, Dale, Lisa Jane and Lisa Marie, and to Steve, my fine son-in-law. They love me, forgive me, and put up with me.

Acknowledgments

I want to thank all the people who filled out a questionnaire or gave me an interview for generously sharing their stories. Also, I thank my son, Andrew, for his critique of the manuscript and Mark Tagge and Richard Tison who helped research. Much credit for this book goes to my mother, Louisa McCormick, who gave me a valuable foundation in relating to people. A special thanks goes to the mothers-in-law and fathers-in-law of my four children who have shown kindness and love to my children, presenting a good example of in-laws.

Table of Contents

✧ *One* ✧

Surviving the
Mother-in-Law Jokes

Which Mother-in-Law Do You Like Better?

✧ **Martha** ✧

"I'm going to come here as often as I want, and I don't need to call first. It's my son's house, and he'll back me up." Martha's challenging tone carried easily from the kitchen into the dining room where her son's wife, Jennifer, stood frozen.

Furious at the brassy assertion of her mother-in-law, she felt her ears turn red with the added embarrassment that Martha said it in front of the entire family assembled in the kitchen. Squelching the desire to turn and run out the front door, Jennifer took a deep breath before returning to the kitchen. She would do her best to act courteously, but inside she no longer cared what her mother-in-law said. She was finished trying to please that woman.

✧ Joan ✧

In another kitchen across the country, a new bride, Debby, nervously prepared her first Thanksgiving meal for her husband's parents. Because his father was an important executive for a large corporation, he and his wife, Joan, traveled world-wide and ate in many famous, gourmet restaurants. Feeling intimidated by their vast culinary experiences, Debby's hands trembled as she worked.

Together the young bride and her mother-in-law, Joan, worked in the little apartment kitchen, putting the finishing touches on the meal and carrying the food to the table.

As Debby began to turn the mashed potatoes into a serving bowl, her hand slipped, dumping the entire contents of the pot on the floor. She stared, horrified, at the white mound. "What can we do?" she groaned. "Everything else will get cold if we make more."

"We'll just scoop them up and eat them." Immediately, the sophisticated mother-in-law stooped to spoon them off the floor and into the serving dish. "We'll not say a word," she whispered, "and no one will ever know."

Debby fell in love with Joan in that instant. This woman, accustomed to servants and surrounded with the beauty of her spacious home, was willing to cover up Debby's disaster, even eat it. Debby felt relaxed and accepted. Joan won a place of love that no succeeding irritation could ever dislodge.

✧ You ✧

Now imagine yourself. The scent of orange blossoms still lingers in the air. The top of the wedding cake rests in a container ready for the freezer. The last guest has departed leaving only the family to finish the cleanup. The candles are all extinguished. They stand in their holders as squat, stubby remnants of their stately beginnings. Your face aglow, you revel in the perfect wedding. When the ring-bearer dropped the cushion, everyone thought it was cute. No one noticed when the mistress of ceremonies mixed up the order for the grandmas' entrance.

Elation fills your heart. But before it can begin to warm you, a more chilling idea invades. Suddenly you are face-to-face with the thought that you tried to avoid as the months of wedding preparations turned to days. Now YOU are a mother-in-law. In the midst of a happy, beautiful event, you became identified with that ignoble creature scorned, despised, and the brunt of endless jokes. You feel like the wedding candles, melted down from the once honored position of motherhood.

Do you swallow hard, knowing you face a fearsome role with the only reward being ire and bad humor directed toward you? Or can you defy the standard lore of mother-in-law? Can you somehow manage to keep your footing on the slippery rocks of this difficult role to reach the peaceful, respectful shore of loving family relationships?

Mother-in-Law Abuse Surrounds Us

Horror stories flood your mind of shipwrecks on the rocky shores of family relationships. No one wants to be the subject of crude humor. You hope your new in-law will not talk about you as you have heard others speak of their mothers-in-law.

In a survey I conducted as background for this book, one woman said, "The best thing my mother-in-law ever did for me was die." Another defined the best quality her mother-in-law possessed—living 840 miles away.

In answer to a question about how often she expected to see her mother-in-law, one young lady replied, "Only when absolutely necessary. I don't want to suffer and be miserable very often."

We cringe at this view of mother-in-law and fervently hope our children's spouses will discontinue this crude legacy. In addition, the inevitable mother-in-law jokes thrust us into a psychological disadvantage. We feel we can't win no matter what we do.

Jokes abound indicating every shade of emotion from irritation to downright malice. Have you ever heard these jokes?

He sent his mother-in-law on a trip to the Thousand Islands and told her to spend a week on each.

Lord Chief Justice Russell said, "The extreme penalty for bigamy? Two mothers-in-law."

This hostile humor reflects the reality of unhappy, broken-down relationships. Yet, I cannot believe that many, if any, mothers-in-law consciously decide to become irritants to their families. It is the unusual woman who sets out to intentionally destroy her contact with her child and his mate.

Personal Note

I distributed a questionnaire to 500 men and women from across the nation, of varied backgrounds, and of age groups ranging from just-married to great-grandparents. From these questionnaires, I learned how much mothers with grown children long for meaningful family contacts. I also learned how much young women desire to establish their own separate family identity. We will explore some of these feelings and opinions as we search for the answers God can supply to our own unique family situations. Sprinkled throughout this book are stories about real people who responded to my questionnaire. The names of the people have been changed in these anecdotes.

They're Married—What's Ahead?

The wedding vows are said and the certificate of marriage is signed; the pair suddenly is a married couple. Any regret a mother may experience over her child's choice or timing will not change that fact. Any amount of persuasion or pressure she exerts against that unit will not change the reality that a marriage has occurred and is a contract in the sight of God, of man, and in the law of our land. But our exertions can certainly change how we are received.

What's a Mother-in-Law to Do?

How can we avoid scarring the lives of our child and spouse? We desire to benefit them. We want to feel loved and appreciated, not blamed. We want a continuing place in the life of this shiny new couple.

Flooding memories fill us of cuddling our child when he was small. We recall sitting up half the night when our daughter was sick, or kissing away the hurt when she fell. Has a life of caring, loving, and sacrificing come to nothing more than enduring bad jokes?

When our child grows up and leaves home, it's normal to feel a sense of loss. We miss the opportunity for impromptu chats, the availability of frequent hugs, and a sense of being needed. The marriage of our child brings changes we can't hold back. We will never return to our previous style of interaction with our child; and, now, we have another person to try to please.

How can a mother-in-law win? One joke says that after you walk down the aisle to take your place in the pew for your child's wedding, it is a good idea to sew your lips shut, then you can't say anything wrong. Will whatever we say be subject to misinterpretation? Do we blunder ahead without giving our role much thought?

As a mother-in-law to three precious girls and one special young man, I know what it is to want their love and acceptance. I understand the fear of being misinterpreted. This book examines the conflicts that can arise in our relationships with our grown children and their spouses, and offers help for solving current problems and preventing future ones. If we already are in troubled relationships, how can we extricate ourselves? Are better relationships possible? I wrote this book for every mother-in-law from the brand-new one to the mother who has worn the role for a long time. Throughout this book I use the pronoun *we* in order to include myself in the advice and admonitions that are suggested. Whether your relationships are smooth and happy or rocky and miserable, each reader will profit from the experiences of others and gain new insights into her own situation.

Every mother-in-law, as she walks away from her child's wedding carrying a paper napkin with those two names permanently engraved on it, wants her name to be etched on their hearts just as firmly. When she tucks her corsage in a plastic bag and refrigerates it to wear the next day, she desires to preserve her relationship with her child more than any perishable flower. She hopes to keep their mutual love fresher.

To preserve a constructive relationship, we will look within ourselves to examine what we can manage, control, and change. We will consider how to best conduct ourselves as mothers-in-law. We will profit from preparing and planning for this role in our lives. We will explore how to protect our loving relationships with our married children and how to survive the title of mother-in-law. We will direct our focus on ourselves, not on what our sons or daughters-in-law could, and should, do to help matters.

Adjust and Adapt

Adjusting and adapting are the keystones of mother-in-law-hood. These traits make it possible to play our role well. By thinking the role through we can become better, in fact, good mothers-in-law. With the help of the Lord and some deliberate examination, we can have in-laws who love us so much they are uncomfortable about laughing over mother-in-law jokes.

Any relationship is a two-way street. It matters significantly what maturity and attitudes your in-law-children have brought with them into your family. But, just as we had no role in making that person what they are, we are not apt to change their character or personality by our intrusive conversation or innuendoes. For harmony's sake, our role in changing that person is best approached by example and prayer.

With God's direction and help, we can adapt and adjust to develop positive, healthy relationships with our grown married children and spouses. If God ordained marriage, then God also ordained this role of mother-in-law. And it stands to reason He will help with anything He ordains. Isaiah 30:21 says, "Your ears will hear a voice behind you, saying, 'This is the way; walk in it.'" There is every reason to believe God is saying the same to us as we walk out our role as a mother-in-law.

Thought before Action

The young married people who responded to my survey expressed appreciation for characteristics that are attainable. We have most of them already. We simply have to find ways to employ them to bless our children. The characteristics that my correspondents noted as irritating or destructive are often overcome by simply realizing the responses these behaviors evoke in the next generation. Awareness and thoughtful evaluation of our role is the biggest step in becoming a beloved mother-in-law.

As the older person in the equation of our children and their spouses, we, as the mother-in-law, have experienced the grace of God longer. We benefit from more experience and have practiced personal relationships longer. Since we have, hopefully, the greater maturity, we can do the most giving and compromising. We can adjust ourselves to what makes the relationship work.

✧ **Rosa and Maria** ✧

Eyes flashing with a mixture of anger and fear, Rosa lay in the labor room gripping her mother-in-law's soft hand. "Why does Juan's unit have to be out at sea now, of all times!"

Juan's mother, Maria, patted Rosa's hand, murmuring sympathetically. The daughter-in-law looked at the prim woman by her side. Anybody else, she thought, I'd rather have anybody else coaching me for this birth. She is so controlled, and I'm losing control fast.

Another contraction and all thoughts of being ladylike before her mother-in-law fled as her moans turned to screams. Soon her yells ceased to express the frustration of Juan's absence. Her discomfort overwhelmed her. Old habit patterns she

9

thought she was overcoming surfaced, and curses hurled down the hall.

A short time later, cuddling her baby daughter, Rosa looked at her husband's mother and tried to find words to apologize for her indelicate vocabulary.

"Thank you," Maria spoke first, leaning over the bed. "Thank you for letting me participate in the birth of this gorgeous little granddaughter. I'm so proud of you bearing her for us. I love you, Rosa."

As Maria gave Rosa a kiss, the new mother took one of her mother-in-law's fingers and curled the baby's fist over it. She smiled, relieved. She did not need to say anything.

Cultivate Godliness

Second Peter 1:5-6 gives characteristics that will contribute to our success as a good mother-in-law. Goodness, knowledge, self-control, perseverance, and godliness will help us satisfy all the people in our lives. Our in-laws should be no exception. A mother-in-law relationship is one that may require work to establish and sacrifice of time and energy to maintain; but, like anything else requiring effort, the results are worth the price. All of us can collect cherished stories about our experiences with our grown children such as Joan with the mashed potatoes at the beginning of this chapter.

Naomi is the classic example of a good mother-in-law. She did not demand the devotion Ruth gave her. Ruth responded voluntarily to go with Naomi. Naomi must have been doing something right to inspire such loyalty from Ruth. The devotion Ruth displayed toward Naomi is the kind of reward we would like to glean from our in-laws. And we can.

Even in extremely negative situations with in-laws, God can teach us to adapt. We will consider discouraging and disheartening situations in a chapter by that name. In the meantime, we will address the normal situation of a married couple with their quirks and shortcomings relating to a normal woman with her quirks and shortcomings, who now is a mother-in-law.

Solutions begin with developing a new style of relationship with our adult child and laying aside our expectations. Beginning cautiously in the first year, we practice controlling our tongue and forgiving mistakes. While taking the time and trouble to learn what pleases and displeases our in-laws and grandchildren, we develop our own separate interests. Even in discouraging situations and through the heartache of divorce, God will help us. We can defy the mother-in-law jokes and enjoy happy relationships.

- ✧ Marriage is a contract with God.
- ✧ Our role is different now.
- ✧ Change ourselves, not our in-laws.
- ✧ Do the most adjusting as the older person.
- ✧ Consciously consider our actions.
- ✧ Strive for godly qualities.

✧ *Two* ✧

Accepting a Mother's Ultimate Goal— To Become Unemployed

✧ *Lisa and Hank* ✧

"Hurry up with the dishes, Lisa. Mom gets antsy if I'm much later than 7:00."

"I know." Lisa scrubbed harder at the crust on the skillet. *"As soon as it gets dark, my folks begin to listen for my car in their driveway."*

A soft sigh escaped her lips. "Do you ever wish we could just stay here on our own farm in the evening?"

"Wouldn't be worth the fuss." Hank grabbed a dish towel, picking up the skillet to dry. *"I've already checked the animals. Everything in the barn is all set for the night."*

After draping the towel over the rod, Hank put

his arm around Lisa, and they left the house. Hank kissed her and opened the car door. For a moment she clung to him; but, by now, the pattern was too well established to break. She let go, climbed in her car, and followed Hank who drove his car to the end of the driveway. He waved as he turned left down the road. She blew a kiss as she turned right to her parents' farm.

For years the long arm of control from their parents precluded a normal household. At dusk each day the married couple left their farm for the homes of their respective parents, who never let go. By the time the parents died, the marriage had lost its passion and become a convenient arrangement. It's unbelievable but true.

✧ *Margaret and Jeffrey* ✧

"The baby's crying." Margaret's husband nudged her and pulled his pillow over his head.

With a groan Margaret swung her feet over the side of the bed. "I was sleeping so deeply, I didn't even hear the baby. I guess the first day home from the hospital wore me out more than I knew." She pattered in to nurse Jeffrey.

"Sweet baby," Margaret crooned over him. She stroked the creases in his chubby leg. "You are the joy of my life, little Jeff."

After a possessive hug, Margaret lifted the baby up in her hands stretching him toward the ceiling. "Here, God, he's yours. Thank you for sending him, but help us to remember he's really yours. I give him back into your hands."

Often, in times of crisis, Margaret remembered that small exercise. The culmination of her one action and her many memories of that action came when he was grown, and she surrendered Jeff to his new wife.

Unemployed? Congratulations!

When your child is grown, congratulations are in order. You have worked yourself out of a job. As our children grew, did we always remember our goal as a mother is to become unemployed? Sometimes our hopes make it hard to turn our children loose, to cease our rearing job, and to stop intruding in their adult lives. Let's look at the first step to good in-law relationships, accepting the independence of our adult child.

Motherhood's Objectives

What is the ultimate purpose of rearing our children anyway? First, we work to help them develop a strong relationship with Jesus Christ as Savior and Lord. Second, we work to enable them to care for themselves and live independently.

To reach the second goal, we grow increasingly less necessary to them while they become increasingly more responsible for their own happiness. That includes their establishing their own goals, not blindly following our agenda for them. For example, an important goal for our children is healthy bodies. To that end we monitored their sleep, taught them the food groups, encouraged exercise, and made sure they brushed their teeth. Now that they are grown, we've turned these responsibilities over to them. No amount

15

of nagging on our part is going to change their approach to their health habits, but it can arouse ire and animosity toward us and resistance to the very goals we hoped to encourage. The same principle is true with other areas of development.

We are successful parents when our child can establish a goal, determine what steps are necessary to reach it, and exert the discipline to take those steps. Ultimately, our children choose their own paths. As deeply as we understand our children, we are not the final judge of what our grown children need for happiness. God is.

They Don't Need You? Good Job!

Since the ultimate goal of parenthood is unemployment, we aim for our child to become self-sufficient and God-dependent, not parent-dependent. Does your grown child dare assume the responsibilities of establishing his own home? Rejoice in your success. Pat yourself on the back instead of regretting your loss. You aimed for this loss all along. The fact the child is stable and mature enough to desire to leave home and marry is a sign of a job well done.

They Don't Owe Us Anything

Making a mature, grown person from a squalling baby necessitates sacrifices. These sacrifices demand not only financial and material resources, but they require the depths of our energies and emotions.

In spite of all the trials and sacrifices that went into their rearing, all our kids owe us is respect. The debt a child owes us for rearing him will be paid, not to us, but to the next generation as he raises his own family. A servant serves without expecting a reward. It is his job. The same goes for parents. For serving our children during their formative years, our reward is their happy, stable lives.

When our children marry, the sacrifices do not end. The ultimate sacrifice, releasing them, is required with the marriage of our child.

We Change Our Role

✧ *Pat and Ralph* ✧

"Slow up! You're over the speed limit," Ralph's mother, Pat, shrilled as she peered at the speedometer.

Satisfied when the car slowed, she leaned back in her seat missing Ralph's mutter, "I hate driving that carping, old woman around."

Neither did she hear the old replay her comment started inside Ralph's mind. "Stop this car and let me drive if you can't do any better than that!" Shouting, Ralph's father had taken over the wheel numerous times in Ralph's sixteenth year. Each occasion left Ralph churning inside and feeling inadequate. The old emotions reared up now, and were transferred readily to his mother.

Ralph's wife, Molly, soon adopted his attitude toward Pat to Pat's bewilderment. "I'm always nice to Molly. Why is she so cool to me?"

The in-law is quick to make the spouse's resentments his own. If we mistreat our grown child in some way and he has angry or hurt feelings, they will be communicated to the spouse. Since our child has married, every interaction with our child directly involves and affects an additional person—our child's marriage partner. Therefore, we cannot be the type of mother we were before. Genesis 2:24 says, "For this reason a man will leave his father and mother and be united to his wife, and they will become one flesh." Becoming one in body involves becoming one in mind, also. Our goal as a mother is to facilitate our child's leaving and cleaving, physically and emotionally, to the new spouse.

Raising youngsters, we are constantly building character, molding a personality, creating an asset to the world. When they marry our principle role changes. No longer in the molding business, we become encouragers.

Do the kids seem unfinished, removed from the oven too soon? Pray! Then compliment what they are doing well. Surely, we can find something pleasing. God will continue the lifetime process of maturing our children. When we, the parents, linger as child developers, we attack the child's self-esteem. Our correcting and cajoling cause our adult child to remember when he failed to please us long ago. Memories of failure, past or present, harm self-esteem. Because our comments caused the loss of self-worth, any resentment aroused is directed at us.

It helps us let go of the developing role to remember Psalm 127:1. "Unless the LORD builds the house, its builders labor in vain. Unless the LORD watches over the city, the watchmen stand guard in vain." Now, it is up to God to build their house and not us.

Keep Alert for Areas Hard to Release
Schooling and Training

✧ *Bernice* ✧

A dismal scene recurred night after night in the bedroom of an eighteen-year-old boy.

"Wallace, we planned and saved all these years for you to go to an Ivy League school. Your brilliant mind should study law, but Louise is distracting you. Stop seeing her," Wallace's mother, Bernice, pleaded, her voice choked with tears.

"But Mom, I love Louise, and she loves me. She won't keep me from using my abilities. Anyway, I don't want to study law."

"You would enjoy law if you gave it a try. We will stand against Louise with all our strength and determination."

As it happened, Bernice's strength and determination cost her ten years of meaningful contact with her son. The thwarted boy ran away, joining the army to support and marry Louise. Bernice ignored Louise as if she did not exist. Finally, when the couple adopted a little girl ten years later, the breech was mended. Fortunately, Bernice had a forgiving daughter-in-law who put all the hurts aside.

Clinging to ambitions for our child's schooling can prevent us from letting go. Any goal established to fulfill ourselves through our child is a trap. Once the job of rearing our tender little ones into adulthood is accomplished, the approaches we used as mothers to achieve these aims are no longer appropriate for our adult children. Reminding, cajoling, and correcting are no longer suitable.

Occupations

✧ *Diane* ✧

"If you hadn't pushed yourself on Bob, he would choose the career God intended for him. You're keeping my son from being a priest." Diane fumed under the stately oak tree in the center of the college campus where Bob had recently given Janice her engagement ring.

Janice stared in disbelief at her future mother-in-law before she threw Bob a bewildered look. "Priest!"

Bob flushed, "Yeah, Mom always talked about that, but I never figured it mattered to her."

"If it weren't for Janice, you would study for the priesthood," Diane repeated her disappointment.

Gritting her teeth, Janice managed to keep the tears behind her eyes from overflowing.

As the years passed, gritted teeth developed into the hallmark of her relationship with her mother-in-law. Diane persisted in dotting her conversations with references to Bob's lost career, not letting go of her disappointment. It simmered just under the surface of her relationship with Janice suffocating warmth between them. Both were cheated.

Stories abound about young men pressured to join the family business, or to take up the family profession. Sometimes the pressures stem from parents longing to fulfill a dream for affluence or prestige through the child. Some grown children flounder unfulfilled in a profession where they don't fit.

Holding goals and challenges before a child for consideration is fine; however, Bernice and Diane went beyond encouragement making their sons' life purposes their own. The unwillingness to let go of a hope long treasured for a child cheated them both out of some happy family times. The cost was greater than the value of the goal.

Time Together

✧ Lib and Patty ✧

At every visit Lib said to her son and daughter-in-law, Patty, "You never come to see me."

"One of these days that is going to be true. I'll live up to what you say and not come anymore," Patty retorted, at last.

Regardless of how short the interval between visits, Lib routinely said every time Patty and her son visited, "You would never know I had a child living in town for all you come to see me."

Their answer to her demands was to come less often, thereby reducing their exposure to the tug of war. As in every tug of war, one side is bound to lose. Guess who loses.

We prevent disappointment when we relinquish what we expect about the amount of time we will spend with our married child and when we keep our expectations small and Christ centered. Psalm 62:5

(KJV) tells us that our expectations belong in God. When they are firmly planted in Him, then it is His pleasure to give us treasures beyond our expectations. We are never disappointed because Jesus has limitless ways to bless us that are far beyond the abilities of our children. "And my God will meet all your needs according to his glorious riches in Christ Jesus" (Philippians 4:19). These riches can include unexpected treats of family togetherness and harmony. He manages those blessings better than we manage them for ourselves.

Our Practical and Emotional Needs

✧ Kathy ✧

"Hello," Jill whispered into the receiver, out of breath from rushing to pick up the phone on only one ring.

"May I please speak with Pete?" his mother, Kathy, asked.

Jill glanced at the clock which read 10:00 a.m. "Pete is in bed asleep, Mom," Jill cupped her hand around the mouthpiece to try to soften the sound of her voice. "Remember he works from 2:00 to 9:00 a.m."

"Oh, yes, that's right," Kathy hesitated only a moment, "but I need him this morning. The rain last night made the vegetable garden just right to weed, and we need his help. May I speak with him, please?"

"The rain would make that job easier today, Mom, but I am not going to wake him up. He's exhausted and wants to get his sleep early today

so he can be awake for parent night at school this evening. Then he needs to be rested enough to get up again at 2:00 a.m. tomorrow morning."

"But we need Pete's help."

"He helped yesterday, Mom. We'll see if he has time when he wakes up."

Jill hung up quickly before her mother-in-law could respond. She liked Pete's mom, but the constant expectation that Pete would continue to do all the things he had done around his parent's house before his marriage was beginning to strain her good will toward the woman.

Letting go is much easier when we don't expect our children to perform chores or errands for us. Our children may meet none, some, or many of our needs. Also, by not expecting our adult children to meet any measure of our emotional needs, what they do meet is a pleasant surprise. Best of all, they aren't burdened trying to supply our happiness.

✧ *Mildred and Linda* ✧

Linda stared blankly at a magazine. She could hear the steady gush of her mother-in-law's animated voice from the next room where she and Linda's husband, Stuart, were conversing. Straining, Linda could not understand Mildred's words. She debated marching onto the sun porch and thrusting herself into the conversation. Instead, she flipped another page, trying to convince herself she was glad Stuart and his mom enjoyed talking together.

"A private chat," Mildred had said when she took Stuart by the arm and practically dragged him out of the room.

What are they talking about that I shouldn't hear, Linda wondered.

As a new bride, still developing her own communication bridges with Stuart, she felt threatened. After a few years, she developed security about her place in her husband's heart and no longer resented their talks; in fact, she made time for them.

Many responses in my survey showed a spouse felt threatened at the beginning of the marriage if the partner's attachment to parents was perceived as very strong.

A challenging sacrifice is giving up a measure of our children's emotional involvement in our lives. Since we first curled their tiny fingers around ours after their delivery, our emotions are entwined closely with them. This entwining never uncurls from around our hearts. But severing the demands that those emotions make on their hearts frees them to respond to us voluntarily. Their adult emotions require disentangling from ours enough to allow them to make another commitment, one binding them to their spouse stronger than to us. The child need not decrease his love for us. Our sacrifice merely releases him from the obligations of that love to perform the obligations that go with his new commitment of emotions.

Children are not designed to meet their parents' emotional needs. A child is designed to create a future for the world, to go forward in time. We release him from our hang-ups to go on into his future. Our children were not created to rectify what has gone wrong in our life, a burden not intended for the next generation to bear. It takes too much energy and time away from what God created him to contribute in his own life-span, to his own generation.

To find the roots of desiring our children to meet our needs, ask yourself these questions. A "yes" to any of these questions can cause us to expect too much from our child.

- ✧ Are we looking for our child to fill in where our husband has failed to meet our need?
- ✧ Do we lack friends to share our burdens and joys?
- ✧ Does child-rearing provide our only sense of accomplishment?
- ✧ Is this need one God wants to fill Himself?

There are needs designed into all of us that only Jesus can meet. God planned it this way on purpose to encourage us to lean on Jesus more than we lean on any human, regardless of that person's place in our lives. Husbands, friends, and children will fail us, but Jesus will not fail us. We probably require a certain amount of failure from people to spur us on to deepen our relationship with Jesus. We want to help our children's emotional health, and not hinder it. Placing the burden of meeting our emotional needs on our children is an inappropriate load for them.

Fears

Desiring the best for our child and fearing something will hinder their happiness often lies behind our inability to let go. When our children marry, it's time to turn the outcome of our hopes and fears over to our child and to the Lord, trusting what we have already molded into them to suffice to bless their lives. We need to believe that wherever we have failed, God will take up the slack in His own superior way. "I sought the LORD, and he answered me; he delivered me from all my fears" (Psalm 34:4).

Naturally we want our children's lives to progress smoothly and happily, and to reflect well on us as parents. These desires tempt us to exert control over their adult decisions, actions, or attitudes. The root of the need to control arises from fear. "For God did not give us a spirit of timidity, but a spirit of power, of love and of self-discipline" (2 Timothy 1:7).

Trusting God provides the antidote to fear. If our children complain we try to tell them what to do. If we detect a desire to guide and direct our grown youngsters, the remedy lies in concentrating on growing in trust of the Lord. "'For I know the plans I have for you,' declares the LORD, 'plans to prosper you and not to harm you, plans to give you hope and a future'" (Jeremiah 29:11). The more we understand His love for us and His goodness toward us, the easier it is to trust Him.

Where Is Our Treasure?

It is easy for us to make our children idols in our

lives if we focus too tightly on them. Matthew 6:21 says, "For where your treasure is, there your heart will be also." If our child becomes the treasure of our heart ahead of the Lord, we have trouble cooperating with God's plan for the progression of life's stages. The danger is our heart will resist progressing to the next stage, the stage of giving up our child. If, as our children are growing, we nourish the treasure of our relationship with God, then our spiritual treasury will be large enough by the time our children marry that we can allow God to help us let them go.

After years of deriving satisfaction from meeting our children's needs, we can feel less important when they no longer require us. We can subconsciously cling to our former role by trying to exert control here and there. In actuality, we are only seeking to feel needed.

As parents we hope our married children have mental stability, healthy habits, a successful marriage, joyful parenting, and salvation that yields to Christ's Lordship. We want them to be successful in all their relationships with their spouse, friends, and co-workers.

Mom's Solutions

Avoid Pressuring the Couple

✧ *Joanne* ✧

"John, you need to take some night courses. Study to get ahead. Make your boss see you're ambitious." John's mother, Joanne, *hammered regularly at her son.*

What she did not know, and John was not about

to tell her, was that his young wife, Chrissy, was afraid of being alone in the evening. John wanted to wait until Chrissy felt more secure before starting classes. The more Joanne tried to spur him, the less John felt like taking her suggestion. Finally, he rejected a good idea entirely.

Unintentionally, we mothers can apply pressure to the marriage. Sometimes we see our children on a collision course with unhappiness. We know that they are sure to crash over the guard rail to disaster if they continue their course. With our added years of experiences, we recognize that certain goals will eventually seem hollow and empty. There are times when we know their pathway will never take them to their declared goal. But our insight does not change the fact that when they are grown, we are no longer the one who brings about their goals. We want them to find peace and joy in their lives, but the best way to see that happen is to hand over the ways and means department to the Lord.

Persistent Prayer

✧ *Anne* ✧

Jim was jeopardizing his marriage to Barbara by continuing a habit formed in bachelor days. Every evening after work, he stopped at a local restaurant for coffee and conversation with his friends. Barbara, feeling neglected, grumbled to Jim's mother, Anne. After pointing out Barbara's feelings to Jim, Anne realized he resisted her counsel. She stopped speaking to Jim and began to speak to the Lord about it.

To Anne's amazement, soon several of Jim's buddies married and stopped coming to the restaurant. Barbara found her voice and expressed her objection directly to Jim. The proprietor of the restaurant even commented, "Get home to your wife." God solved the problem, and Anne still had her relationship with Jim.

Prayer is a more effective means of seeing our adult child attain the happiness of successful living than all our lectures, criticisms, and well-intended comments. Well-calloused prayer knees serve our grown children best.

Think of Them as Adults

If our children live away from home before they marry, it's easier to practice elevating our children to adulthood in our thoughts. If our child lives in our home until he marries, we will have to watch our thoughts, requiring ourselves to regard them as adults.

Instead of dwelling on the loss of our former role in their lives, we rejoice in the lessening of responsibilities. Our burden is released when we give the responsibility for our grown children's lives to the capable care of God. "Every good and perfect gift is from above, coming down from the Father of the heavenly lights, who does not change like shifting shadows" (James 1:17). We need to remind ourselves that our child is not our child, but a precious gift loaned to us for a short time. God helps us release control, be slow to speak, and keep peace with our grown children. When we fail, all we need to do is apologize and begin again. We moms keep wearing our alert bonnet because sometimes we forget our ultimate goal is to let go. Our goals change from developing our child to encouraging him.

- ✧ Aim, as we raise our children, to become unemployed.
- ✧ Free our children from owing us for raising them.
- ✧ Be an encourager rather than a developer.
- ✧ Let go of our married child.
- ✧ Give our fears to God.
- ✧ Elevate our married child to an adult in our thinking.

✧ *Three* ✧

Releasing Expectations

✧ **Lois and Darlene** ✧

"Finish your tea, Darlene, we need to decide what you will wear tonight."

Darlene's hands shook just thinking about the party planned to introduce her to her fiance Larry's family and friends during this first visit to Larry's home since her engagement.

She hastily swallowed her tea and followed her future mother-in-law, Lois, to the room where Darlene's suitcase lay open. One by one Darlene pulled out the dresses she had brought for the visit. They were her favorites, ones she felt comfortable wearing. Soon she began to feel quite uncomfortable.

"That's too casual." Lois frowned at the first dress. *"My friends would think you were brazen if you wore that short dress,"* Lois tossed the

second garment on the bed. On and on the dismissal of each dress was pronounced.

"Look." Lois threw open the closet door. "I put some dresses in here that Larry's cousin passed along. Let's find one to project the right image tonight."

"But that's not me," Darlene protested as her future mother-in-law pulled out a black, velvet gown.

"But it is us, dear," Lois replied and moved up close to look at Darlene's face. "We'll need to get you some more eye shadow and mascara."

"I don't really like to wear makeup."

"You'll get used to it," Lois insisted. "It's a shame your hair is so dark. I always thought Larry would marry a blond." She pulled a strand between her fingers. "It is much too long, but I suppose it is too late to correct that now."

A chill ran through Darlene. I'm not what she wants for her son, she thought. Even as she pulled her hair back from her future mother-in-law, she began to pull away inside, to build a wall between them.

❖ Caroline and Sarah ❖

Caroline gave her daughter-in-law a college catalogue, carefully marked to draw attention to the nursing courses.

"Thanks," Sarah accepted the book and leafed through it. "I'm registering to major in art next week."

"Art?" her mother-in-law exclaimed. "You can't

make any money in that. Nurses are always needed. Try nursing."

"But Mother Caroline, I get faint at the sight of blood."

"You can get over that. You need to help Randy with expenses."

Clashing Expectations

Lois's expectations about the type of girl her son would marry caused disappointments and difficulties. Accepting our in-laws the way they are when they marry our child lays a good foundation for a relationship. Obviously, our child was attracted to them. Caroline's expectations that her son's wife would work outside the home and provide significant income produced strained relationships. Most of us have expectations in many areas; we just aren't aware of them. These expectations influence our relationship with our in-laws.

Our expectations for relating to our adult children come from many sources: from our own childhood, from our reading, from our relationship with our own parents after we married, from our friends' children, sometimes even from TV or daydreams.

Meanwhile, your child has developed his own set of expectations about married life—how he or she will relate to you, the mother. Then, there are the expectations your child's spouse brings to the marriage. In addition, your child's spouse has parents who come conditioned with their own notions.

These various ideas of married life and how all the people involved are to relate to one another are unlikely to agree completely. Unrealistic expectations are doomed to disappointment. Sometimes, expectations are legitimate, but they don't match the reality of our situation. When two people have different expectations about the same subject, there is a clash.

Realistic Expectations

When our children marry, thinking of this word picture can help us give our in-law proper place. It is a bit like a spool of thread. While the thread is wound tightly on the spool it cannot integrate into a piece of material. As it is unwound from the spool where it has been closely wrapped, it is free for sewing into a piece of fabric forming a garment. If we parents are the spool and the garment is a marriage, it is necessary to free the thread, our child, from the spool to allow it to integrate with the fabric and form a garment. One important expectation we bring to our children's marriages is that they will become less attached to us and more attached to their mates. With that realistic expectation, we hurt less and prepare for the essential drawing away which is important for the new marriage to become strong.

Since our children really belong to God, we moms can expect to give up our emotional claims on them when they are grown. Because of God's principle of relinquishment, what we give up God returns to us. When we relinquish our married child, God will return to us a new relationship of a different nature, but equally precious. A key to success in our relationship with our in-laws is to give up our own child as completely as we can and, with the help of our Lord, more completely than our natural ability would allow us.

A finely tuned antenna in our child's mate picks up the degree we let go of our child. To the measure they sense that our hold is still there, they will enter into a conscious or a subconscious struggle with us over our child. This puts the one we love so much into a difficult position. Our child feels like a taut rope in a tug of war.

Send Them Off—Geographically and Emotionally

Genesis says that a man shall leave his father and mother and cleave to his wife, meaning emotionally as well as geographically. Think of Rebekah's parents in Genesis. Her parents had not even met the man who was sending for their daughter. In Genesis 24:55 Rebekah's family asked for her to stay a few more days. Their request speaks a volume of emotional implications. When she left, her family probably never saw her again. Perhaps they only heard from her indirectly once in a long while through the news of some caravan. Yet the family sent her with a blessing. Genesis 24:60 says, "And they blessed Rebekah and said to her, 'Our sister, may you increase to thousands upon thousands; may your offspring possess the gates of their enemies.' "

Summoning up our courage, we do the same if our children live in some far-flung place. Even if they are living close to us geographically, emotionally, we allow them to move away from us. Emotionally, we send them off as completely as Rebekah's parents did.

✧ *Betty* ✧

"Let me show you a neat way to fold sheets,"
Betty said volunteering to unload her daughter-in-
law, Joyce's, clothes dryer. "But first hand me that
broom, and I'll get the dust out from behind the
dryer."

Joyce laughed and handed her the broom. She
never took offense at anything Betty said or did.

Her mother-in-law had taken an unusual approach
by moving out of state after her son's marriage in
order to free the new couple to develop their marriage
apart from her. An extreme step, but it assured Joyce
that her mother-in-law was motivated to help, not
criticize or hinder. Could we mentally move out of the
way and bring the same benefits?

Have we assumed our children will live near by? Did
they move away instead? Every evaluation we form
about life is relative. We can choose to look for the
best, or we can nurse regrets. Choosing the optimistic
approach helps us adapt and adjust to the reality in
our lives.

For instance, if our children live in town, thankfulness that we can see them easier is the antidote to
regret that we are not seeing them as often as we
might like. Praise the Lord they are readily accessible
sometimes.

If our children *do* live in far-flung places, we can be
grateful that they are living. Being grateful for this
obvious truth helps us keep our perspective and
emotional balance. Although it's wrenching for us to
see a child move away, the best approach is accept-

ing the situation gracefully and looking for the bright side. With the couple away, there will be less chance to fail as a mother-in-law.

Areas Where Expectations Can Snare Us
The Wedding

✧ Patty and Dan ✧

Patty sat in the decorated car, nervously brushing rice from her bridal gown. With her radiance dimming and her hairdo wilting, she waited alone in the hot car.

"Dan, you can't leave before saying goodbye to your guests and thanking them for coming," Dan's mother said as she grabbed his arm after he helped Patty into the get-away car.

"Thanks for coming," Dan shouted at the milling wedding guests, waving an arm in farewell.

But that would not do. Mother firmly tugged him over to the nearest group of people and on to the next "to perform his duty" as she put it. Thirty minutes later he joined his steaming bride in the car and zoomed away into the traffic, where Patty's screech of frustration with her mother-in-law fell only on his ears.

The wedding is a dangerous arena for the mother-in-law. Some control is often required on the part of the bride's mother to ensure an affordable, smooth event, but resentments aroused can linger long after the guests have gone home. Our intention not to control after the wedding is the important impression to convey. The wedding is a moment in time; our relationship is for a lifetime.

Ginny battled for years to forgive her mother-in-law. Because of the woman's strident opposition to her son marrying Ginny, the groom's four sisters didn't attend the wedding. They were afraid to experience the aftermath of their mother's wrath. Only after Ginny gave her resentment to God did a happy relationship begin to develop between her and her mother-in-law.

If your child's wedding has not yet taken place, be sure to refer to Appendix 2 in the back of this book for more practical help during the crucial engagement days.

Holidays

✧ *Florence and Hattie* ✧

"I'm missing the kids, and they haven't left the reception yet." Florence held a fist full of rice as she waited for her son and his bride, Latisha, to make a run for the wedding car which was festooned with crepe paper and whipped cream.

"Me too," Latisha's mother, Hattie, agreed clutching her rice. "I can't wait until Christmas."

"Christmas is ours this year. We have the whole family every other year so all our ten kids who are scattered across the country can be together. This is our year. Next year is the spouse's year. You can have them next Christmas," Florence said.

Hattie stared. When the bridal car disappeared in the traffic, her clenched fist still gripped the now clammy rice, her smile turned upside down.

We can understand Hattie's feeling. Gulping, my husband and I released our children to make their own holiday plans. Although we hope for whole family celebrations sometimes, we understand the tugs caused by loyalty toward two families. The children have enough tension blending their two backgrounds without us applying pressure.

Florence's family needed a system for reunions, but flexibility is key to the in-law role. Each family requires its own unique solutions to holidays, ones everyone can accept. At times we may need to readjust those solutions as grandchildren are born, families move, and grandparents age. As our immediate family changes we need to remind ourselves that our in-laws families change as well. Perhaps our in-laws need to accommodate someone on their side. We need to remain flexible throughout our lives.

Social Life

✧ *Alice* ✧

"I've arranged to have Dick's birthday party Saturday. Would you rather have it start at five or six?" Dick's mother, Alice, bubbled into the phone.

Dick's new wife, Rachel, clapped her hand over the receiver before muttering, "I'd rather you did not have it at all." She struggled to make her voice pleasant as she answered her mother-in-law. "I'd planned a cozy, candlelight dinner for two as Dick's celebration."

"But our family always gets together for birthday celebrations. We are a close family."

Rachel actually enjoyed their family times, but

she found herself resisting more and more. She thought her mother-in-law, Alice, wanted to maintain the original family unit of seven just as it was before the marriage, simply adding her as the eighth member to the family. She resisted Alice until she knew the woman had released the hope that life would go on with no alteration to the original family unit. Not feeling the need to assert herself anymore, Rachel's relationship with Alice blossomed into a loving one that is extremely satisfying to them both.

✧ **Wanda and Tricia** ✧

"My mother-in-law arranges too many events for us. We never have time to plan outings we might enjoy on our own, because she's already bought tickets or made promises on our behalf," Wanda complained.

"My mother-in-law interrogates us regularly; she wants to know every single, tiny thing we do. Every week, she expects us to outline our plans for her," Trisha commented. "I really don't mind her knowing where we are going and when, but I mind her thinking it's her right to know. We don't have any privacy."

✧ **Esther** ✧

"Hurry, Billy! Grab your Boy Scout handbook and run to the car. Grandma's telephone call will come before I can get back home." Carol accelerated as fast as she dared through the Atlanta traffic, trying to drop Billy off and return home *before her mother-in-law called.*

"Here she is now, Mother." Carol's husband motioned to her when she returned.

"Hello, Mother Esther," Carol spoke breathlessly into the phone. "Yes, yes, I know you always call at 7:30 Tuesdays, but you know Boy Scouts also meet every Tuesday. Of course, I want to talk to you, but at least you had Hugh on the phone before I came.

"Well, no, we can't get them to change the Scout meeting. Of course I'm glad you call every week, but I'm sure you're also glad Billy enjoys Scouts." Although Carol's voice stayed sugar sweet, she made a face into the phone.

We aren't always aware of all the pressures in our children's adult lives. Giving them control of their social lives and timetables will help reduce these pressures.

Affection and Time

"My mother-in-law demands we spend time with her. Ordinarily I enjoy her company, but when I must visit to prove I love her, I don't feel like going," Jill told me. Everyone is happier when we don't evaluate their love for us by the time they spend with us.

Even if the couple wants to spend time with us, sometimes their desire cannot be translated into action due to the time pressures in their lives. Chances are they'll fit us in now and again; however, demanding their time and affection will not cause it to happen.

Christian Life and Behavior

✧ Peter and Nancy ✧

"Don't answer it." Peter rolled over. Sleepily he draped his arm over Nancy as the phone rang insistently.

"It's 8:30." Nancy reached for the phone.

"It's your mother every Sunday morning," Peter said in disgust. She wants to wake us up. She figures if we are awake, we'll decide we might as well get up and go to church today."

"Guess we can fool her." Nancy giggled and turned away from the phone to snuggle close to Peter. "Church can wait a little for us."

✧ Leslie and Pauline ✧

It's early, Leslie thought as she drove home from her meeting. On the spur of the moment, she veered off her course to drive the few miles to her daughter, Pauline's house.

Maybe I should have called first from the church, she thought as she mounted the steps to the front door and rang the bell.

"Hi," Leslie greeted her daughter who answered the door. "I was near so I thought I'd—" She didn't finish the sentence because her eye fell on her son-in-law, Jimmy.

There he sat with a cigarette in one hand and a cocktail in the other. "Hi, Mom," he said, then downed the rest of his drink.

"Jimmy, I can't believe what I'm seeing. You're smoking and drinking." Leslie stared.

"Yeah," Jimmy stood up, deliberately blowing

smoke at Leslie. "It's our lives, we do what we want." He staggered out of the room, leaving Leslie dumfounded.

It takes the Holy Spirit to change lives. Mothers-in-law rarely do. Even if the young couple's choices leave a lot to be desired in our eyes, if we try to change them, we run the risk of strengthening their resolve to demonstrate independence rather than modify their lifestyle. Prodding won't make church attendance or anything else attractive.

Look at what other people wrote on my questionnaire.

⋄ "My mother-in-law is our spiritual judge. The scripture saying once to die and then the judgment doesn't reckon on my mother-in-law. When she wants to be sure we understand what she's saying is important, she says God said it. God won't have anything left to say to us when we die; she'll have said it all."

⋄ "After my mother-in-law comes, I can count on finding tracts left all over the house," Seth said. "Hinting, always hinting, at what we should or shouldn't do."

⋄ "I try to be a Christian. I hope God is easier to please than my mother-in-law," Graham grimaced. "She makes me feel inadequate."

Living a godly life ranks tops in importance; however, God prefers that our actions spring from a desire to please Him rather than going through spiritual motions like puppets. Pushing and pressing a godly lifestyle on our grown family won't draw them close to God. The pattern of our lives, not pressure, provides the best influence. In fact, pressure may offset the example of our lives. One man told his mother, "Mom, you did a good job. We know what you want for our lives. Don't tell us."

Opinions

Ashley told me she dreaded opening letters from her mother-in-law. The letters were always full of how she should do things. "I skim the letters and dump them in the trash. In person, well, thankfully, she lives too far away to be in person much."

Katlin said she works to remember which topics of conversation are safe with her mother-in-law. Politics are definitely out. There is only one correct political point of view; and if Katlin stumbles into another viewpoint, she can count on heated correction. As a result, her conversations with the woman are bland and non-consequential.

We can make suggestions and present our thoughts as long as it's clear we're only discussing ideas, not trying to dictate. How we approach discussions differs from one couple to another. Their perception of our intent is what matters. Each personality requires different handling. It helps if, before expressing ourselves, we ask, "Are you asking my opinion? Do you want to know what I think?" Unless the answer is yes, swallow the words.

"A fool finds no pleasure in understanding but delights in airing his own opinions" (Proverbs 18:2).

The family doesn't need our opinion on everything. Many opinions are best left unnoted.

Priscilla said, "We keep my mother-in-law in the dark about our lives as much as possible." The more we moms try to control, the less we will know about our family. Censuring our knowledge is one way to undercut our control.

House and Home

✧ Norma and Kay ✧

"I really don't like that style of lamp." Kay tried to be polite as she resisted her in-law's ideas about how she should decorate her home.

"But it's perfect to hang over your dining room table," Norma, her mother-in-law, persisted as they ambled through the furniture store.

"It would look even better if you reversed the location of your sofa and the table."

"I don't want the table on the other wall, because it would not be convenient to the kitchen." With effort, Kay kept her voice even. "The contemporary look is more my style." Kay hoped she was making herself clear.

She was sadly mistaken as the next day proved.

She arrived home from her morning classes at a nearby college tired and wishing she did not have to entertain her visiting in-laws.

She walked through the door and automatically pitched her books toward the dining table. Instead they landed on the sofa. Sure enough, the sofa and the table had been switched along with every other piece of furniture in her living room. To cap it off, over the table hung the country lamp she had rejected in the store.

"Doesn't it look wonderful," Norma gushed. "This is so much better than the other arrangement."

Furious, Kay walked quickly back outside choking down angry words. There she encountered her father-in-law walking to his truck carrying her old lamp under one arm and a metal magazine rack under his other arm.

"What are you doing with my lamp and magazine rack?" Her voice sounded loud and unnatural in her ears.

"I cleaned out your shed and got rid of the junk so you have plenty of room to organize everything."

Kay ran to the shed. "There isn't anything left to organize," she wailed. "Where are my things?"

"I took a load to the dump, and am just about to leave with the second load."

It's hard to believe, but Kay's story is true. Since the couple's home is an extension of themselves, it behooves us to approve it and their operation of it. A couple's home is their domain. We respect their arrangements in it. A family feels defensive about the place where they live. A good precaution limits our conversation about the place to what we approve, ignoring what we disapprove—unless we think we will break a leg in the hole on the front steps.

During a visit Marian shook her napkin out, placed it in her lap and asked, "Are these the only kind of napkins you own? Poor quality." Having sabotaged the atmosphere of that meal, she mailed a set of hand-hemmed napkins as soon as she returned home to insure the home was equipped to her standards.

Another young woman expressed a similar resentment. When her mother-in-law arrived, she marched straight to the television and snapped the on switch. If it was already on, she switched the channel to what she wanted to watch, regardless of how many people were absorbed with the program in progress.

When we are in our children's home, we are guests, and must put on our best manners, even if they are family.

Grandchildren

When we worry about our grandchildren, it's easy to slip into trying to exert control without realizing it. The solution is to cast the children upon God. "Cast your cares on the LORD and he will sustain you; he will never let the righteous fall" (Psalm 55:22).

"My mother-in-law insisted we should have an abortion when I was pregnant with my last child. She was not sympathetic to us thinking God disapproved," Sandy said. "Our solution was to stay away from her until after the baby was born. She still mutters 'too many children' sometimes."

Some subjects, such as how many children and when they arrive, are clearly beyond our business. Only if we are financing the family have we any right to a say-so. Then we have another set of problems on our hands.

Expect from God

We can't lose by releasing all expectations of our children. Our disappointment stems more from what we expect them to do than from what they do.

It helps to have low expectations of what other adults will do for us and high expectations of what Jesus will do for us. If we keep our actions and reactions before the Lord in prayer, we are continually strengthened in not expecting too much from our children. When we are protected from harboring harmful expectations that lead to disappointment or troubled relationships, we can expend more energy interceding for the couple in the areas where we see their needs, struggles, or failures.

- ✧ Accept our in-laws as they are.
- ✧ Remember wedding plans are insignificant in terms of a lifetime.
- ✧ Be flexible about holidays.
- ✧ Remember time does not equal love.
- ✧ Lay our expectations on the Lord and not on people.

✧ *Four* ✧

Getting a Good Start

✧ **Lilly and Rhonda** ✧

"I haven't made the bed yet . . . ," Rhonda's voice trailed off. It was too late. Her mother-in-law, Lilly, walked down the hall with her friend, Marge, in tow.

Embarrassed, Rhonda followed the ladies into her bedroom. *Maybe if I stand in front of the bureau, they won't notice I dumped my powder box this morning and haven't cleaned it,* Rhonda thought.

"Rhonda, it's time to wash your curtains. They're dusty." Lilly gave them a little shake. "I wanted you to see how the bedspread matches the curtains, Marge."

The gall of the woman barging unannounced into my house with someone I don't know and then marching into my bedroom. At least her friend has the decency to look uncomfortable, Rhonda thought.

"Why do you keep your stationery in this drawer?" Lilly asked as she pulled open a drawer by the bed.

Hoping to forestall the woman from throwing open her closet door, Rhonda moved quickly to the bedroom door. "Bring Marge into the living room, and I'll fix you some tea."

Marge had the good sense to head immediately out the door. Lilly followed reluctantly, "I wanted you to see how perfectly everything matches."

✧ *Amy and Colleen* ✧

"Thanks for showing me your Ireland snapshots. They are as good as the postcards you sent." Amy smiled at her mother-in-law, Colleen.

"I brought you a little present. Open it." Colleen waited while Amy tore off the paper.

Amy chortled with delight as she held up a tea cozy. "It's beautiful. Why, it's fancier than the ones you gave your own daughters. Are you sure you meant for me to have this?"

"Of course, my dear, you're as important to the family as anyone else."

Lilly was years overcoming her brassy visit to her daughter-in-law's new home. In contrast, Amy felt accepted because of such a small thing as a souvenir from her in-laws' first trip after Amy's wedding.

Feeling Insecure?

Becoming a new mother-in-law is like driving the bumper cars at the fair. Without a finely responsive steering mechanism, the cars move about knocking into each other. Unsure how to handle these cars, we crash, thud, and bump around.

Uninitiated and unsure as we begin to maneuver with our new in-laws, we will crash less and experience smoother driving by observing principles that help us steer a safer path.

Remember how we felt when we were newlyweds? Remember some of the unthinking responses we had then, responses lacking the understanding we possess now? Over the years, we've grown in maturity. The next generation requires time to grow in relationship skills. While we wait, our understanding is greater if we remember how we responded when we were young. Proverbs 10:23b says, "A man of understanding delights in wisdom." Here are tips for beginning a good relationship based on understanding and consideration.

Love Them First

"We love because he [God] first loved us" (1 John 4:19). By exhibiting love first to our new in-laws, such as Colleen's gift to Amy, we set the groundwork for them to fall in love with us, some sooner, some later. Before we were aware of God's ways, He gave us a beautiful world, sometimes shielded us from consequences of our sin, and demonstrated patience with us. If we ask, He will show us how to exhibit love to our in-laws in ways they can receive. We can win them by proceeding according to God's principles.

Communicate Carefully

"A word aptly spoken is like apples of gold in settings of silver" (Proverbs 25:11). Careful communication supplies an important key to nourishing relationships. Polish communication skills. Develop the habit of double checking whenever you speak of something easily misinterpreted, or easily interpreted as interfering. Ask your family to restate what they think you said. Restate what you think you hear them say. Check if your true intent is coming across. Rephrase what you're saying in several ways with qualifiers thrown in to make sure you aren't misinterpreted.

Be quick to readjust what you're saying after sensing their reaction. Example: "We're having company for dinner Tuesday night and would love to have you join us." A strange look passes across your son-in-law's face. Noticing, you quickly add, "As always if you have other plans, no pressure. We just want you to feel included."

The qualifiers beat dealing with in-law's thoughts such as, "Your parents are always using up our free time."

Or look at this example: "I saw a beautiful bedspread on sale at the store yesterday, I thought it looked like the kind you want. Check it out if you have time." You notice your daughter-in-law's lips become a thin, compressed line. "Maybe it's not what you're looking for," you add, "but I thought of you when I saw it. Thought I'd tell you in case you're interested."

The qualifying statements prevent this reaction, "Why can't your mother let me pick out my own things? Doesn't she understand that we just don't have money to spend on things like that right now?"

Limit comments about choice of clothing, hair style, and physical appearance to complimentary ones. In-laws need acceptance. When a couple first marries, they start out insecure about how well their in-laws like them. They want approval.

Until we learn the spouse's thinking, it is wise to avoid throwing around our opinions too freely. We can step on toes without realizing it. Use caution especially with politics.

Respect Their Ways and Opinions
What Shall We Be Called?

Whatever makes them comfortable. Some young people select a name right away, others experiment. When suggesting a title we like, remember they may have emotional responses attached to the label. Many want to save the name they call their own mom or dad as a special name used for no one else. Whatever the choice, it is not worth an argument. A name spoken in affection is worth more than any name spoken from emotional distance. The choice is theirs.

Get to Know Them

✧ Kate or Dawn ✧

"My mother-in-law is such a help when she comes to visit. She always sorts and straightens out my linen closet. I enjoy the tidy feeling," Kate said gratefully.

53

"My mother-in-law is a nosy and interfering woman," Dawn said. "When she comes for a visit, she's always straightening up my linen closet. I guess she doesn't think I'm neat enough."

Which daughter-in-law is yours? How does your daughter-in-law view help around the house? It's important to know her views. "Good understanding wins favor" (Proverbs 13:15a).

What pleases this new family member? What creates resentment? We feel our way around until we can answer those questions, and then conduct ourselves accordingly. In what areas are they defensive? Where do they feel secure? Those answers will help us relate in positive ways so that we don't offend, alienate, or antagonize; but rather, we build self-esteem and create harmony.

If there are racial or cultural differences, we need to be careful not to assume they have the outlooks, attitudes, or responses with which we are familiar. Read about the cultural background of your in-law. If possible spend time with the spouse's family members to better understand their approach to life. Seek out an unrelated person of the same background with whom you can become friends. Sometimes it is easier to ask those innocent but uninformed questions of acquaintances rather than relatives.

Realize Methods Differ
✧ *Eileen and Michelle* ✧
Eileen habitually lectured on the proper way to perform chores. "No, no," Eileen remonstrated

while she visited Michelle's home. "Those onions aren't cut up nearly fine enough for the casserole."

After Michelle dutifully minced the onions again and began snapping beans, Eileen gave further instructions, "That's not the way to snap green beans."

"I really didn't think it mattered how green beans were snapped as long as they were in manageable pieces and cooked tastily," Michelle's voice grew testy.

"There's a right way to do everything, and I do mean everything," Eileen stated.

That's not the right way to talk to me, Michelle thought.

After dinner Eileen tried subtle tactics. "There are some people who don't write their thank you notes for a dinner party for days."

Michelle cringed. I guess my letter written a week later flunked the thank you note test.

Young couples frequently mentioned resentment aroused by comments they interpreted as intended to set their thinking or actions straight.

✧ *Lenore and Maggie* ✧

Lenore followed Maggie around the table. As Maggie set it, Lenore rearranged the silver. After dinner Lenore insisted upon feeding Maggie's dog potato chips, candy and beer in spite of Maggie's protests.

Flexibility is a mother-in-law requirement. Each in-law is different. By respecting them and adapting ourselves to their personalities and methods, we help each in-law thrive.

✧ *Tanya and Cecile* ✧

When Tanya measured the oregano carefully for her casserole, Cecile protested, "You aren't going to put that in, are you?"

"Well, I was," Tanya told me, "but I was so upset I dumped it on the counter instead and never did put it in the dish. I didn't enjoy eating the food either."

Better to eat a disliked spice than become disliked. We must let our in-laws know we appreciate their ways, interests, and talents. They are under no obligation to adopt our ways unless they choose. For creating harmony, acceptance beats instruction.

Use Our Best Manners

We have all developed skills for making and maintaining friendships with our peers. Putting the same skills into practice with our new in-laws gains their respect and love.

Remember Lilly at the beginning of the chapter? Drawers, cabinets, and closets are off bounds to in-laws except by invitation. In addition, we can exercise telephone courtesy by asking if it is a convenient time to call. Try to avoid calling at mealtime or when you know they are busy. Remember how you enjoyed cuddling up with your spouse before bedtime? Avoid calls after 9:00 or 10:00 p.m.

Visiting: When to Come, How Long to Stay

"My mother-in-law, Belle, came from Kansas and appeared on our doorstep in Ohio," Beth said. "Dumbfounded and inconvenienced, we did not greet her with enthusiasm. Belle complained about our lack of warmth for years."

More than one person reported surprise visits at awkward times. The surprise boomeranged with a tattered welcome mat. The cardinal rule is to call before going. Good manners dictate calls before visiting. Resist the idea to pop in and "surprise" them. People appreciate the courtesy of time to whoosh the newspapers out of sight or make the bed. Such courtesy seems obvious for out-of-town visits.

Connie accepted her son-in-law's invitation to visit them for a week while the family was in a beach home. The problem? Connie stayed four weeks. She was offended, because she was not invited again. It is better to have a short enjoyable visit and leave while everyone still wishes we could stay.

Visiting: Knock First

Megan was painting a picture for her mother-in-law's birthday gift when the woman barged into the house spoiling the surprise. Manners dictate we knock before entering a neighbor's home. Just because they are our flesh and blood does not exempt our child and mate from this courtesy.

If we haven't called first and they aren't expecting our visit, it is a good idea to knock and wait at the front door. Resist the temptation to peer in the sliding glass door. Many newlyweds can relate stories about how they were embarrassed or how their family members were embarrassed when amorous moments were interrupted.

Accept the Couple's Adjustment Period

The couple will fumble learning how to live with each other just as we fumble learning to relate to them. When we accept their learning period without making unrequested comments, they are less likely to think we judge them. Unless they ask, they will work through their differences better without outside comment. Face it. Now, we are on the outside.

Tell our child our home is open for visits, but it is not a haven of escape from the marriage. Many a marriage floundered because there was a place to flee instead of facing and resolving issues. The couple is forced to search for workable solutions when it is not too easy to escape. The exception to this maxim is abuse in the marriage. (See chapter 12.) Here we address the normal spats a couple experiences as they blend their different backgrounds and personalities together to form a unit.

Make Them Feel Included

✧ Donna and Gloria ✧

"Would you like to spend the first week in October with me in our mountain cottage?" Donna asked her daughter-in-law, Gloria.

"Sounds like fun, but Hugh won't have any vacation days left to take off."

"I know, but I'm asking you. We could have a good time just the two of us."

Gloria told me, *"I felt so special that my mother-in-law wanted to be with me even when she couldn't include her son. We had a relaxed time full of good conversation."*

Audrey was baffled for several years by her sister-in-law's behavior. Violent outbursts, including lamps thrown down stairs or tables overturned, happened right in front of her eyes; yet no one ever offered an explanation. Without any understanding, Audrey was more than a little worried and she felt shut out of the family.

A simple statement about the nature or root of the girl's problem would have helped Audrey's peace of mind. Inclusion even in family heartaches gives the in-law a sense of belonging. Family conversations become frustrating to the new family member if they're missing some piece of information common to the rest of the family. Make the in-laws feel like a true family member by filling in the blanks of family lore. Clue them in on family jokes. While it's not necessary to rattle all the family skeletons, in-laws resent deliberate secrecy.

Daisy's daughter-in-law, Joy, felt included and special in the family. After Joy's surgery, Daisy made the two-hour drive to see her in the hospital. She spent all her time there, returning home without seeing her own son. After that, Joy rested secure in her mother-in-law's affection.

Avoid Comparisons

With Us

"When they measure themselves by themselves and compare themselves with themselves, they are not wise" (2 Corinthians 10:12b).

Remind your child and his intended that you were not always what they see now. When we were first married, I had the monthly pleasure of tossing out from the refrigerator little bowls of black fuzzy blobs which appeared ready to take on lives of their own. I later learned to utilize our food leftovers—much later. Funny stories about our first married days when we learned things the hard way help our new in-laws not to compare themselves with us. This is particularly important with a daughter-in law, because she can feel inadequate when she compares her homemaking skills with our more developed ones.

Instead of trying to protect ourselves from embarrassment, we should reveal bits of our own failures. Shared flubs increase intimacy. Not knowing much about housekeeping when I was first married, I put a lot of wet spaghetti in a paper garbage bag. When my husband carried it out, the bottom broke open on our fire escape stairs. Each string of spaghetti became festooned over a different grid. For what felt like forever, we picked each strand up one by one, laughing later—much later. We sure aren't perfect.

We moms probably peel apples a lot faster than our daughters-in-law, because we have peeled many a bushel more than they, not because we are inherently better apple-peelers.

With Other Family Members

✧ *Phyllis and Shirley* ✧

"You stay so thin, Shirley, while my daughters keep getting plumper," Phyllis said passing her daughter-in-law a plate of Boston creme pie at the family gathering.

Shirley took the plate while trying to avoid looking at her two sisters-in-law. Unable to think of something clever to help their feelings, she stared at her pie. Her already shaky relationship with her new sisters-in-law seemed destined to sour.

The income of various families, the status of their jobs, the levels of their education, or how they spend their money aren't subjects for comparison. Everyone can see the differences for themselves. Comparisons create divisions between the very people we want to draw together. Resist honoring the son-in-law who practices medicine over the one who is an auto mechanic, for instance. "But if you show favoritism, you sin and are convicted by the law as lawbreakers" (James 2:9).

With the In-Law's Parents

Income or educational differences between the two sets of in-laws are also best left unnoted. The desire for a higher social status for our children is a hazardous longing. Acceptance without jealousy or disdain helps most.

Many battles are launched over how much time the young couple spends with the other set of parents. When our child marries, turn off our sensitivity. We can choose whether or not we allow ourselves hurt feelings. Refuse to be hurt.

Psalm 119:165 (KJV) gives us the standard. "Great peace have they which love thy law: and nothing shall offend them." The marriage of our child gives God an opportunity to test the depth of this concept in our lives. We possess the power to choose not to take offense.

First Corinthians 13:7 challenges us with "[Love] always protects, always trusts, always hopes, always perseveres." Let's believe the best about our new in-law and trust the Lord to bring about what we believe.

Getting a good start is important. Women from all ages responded to my questionnaire. Even the ladies in their eighties remembered crystal clear the infractions of their mothers-in-law. Word for word they quoted offending phrases. If elephants have good memories, daughters-in-law do also. Some of them etch our mistakes permanently into their brains.

As we honor our in-laws with respect and genuine interest in them, extending courtesy, a meaningful and significant relationship will begin to grow.

- ✧ Help our in-laws feel secure in our love and acceptance.
- ✧ Take time to get to know them and respect our in-laws' desires and thinking.
- ✧ Use our best manners.
- ✧ Avoid comparisons.
- ✧ Refuse to take offense.

✧ 𝓕𝒾𝓿𝑒 ✧

Controlling Our Tongue

✧ **Carmen** ✧

"Come in, Mom." Choly balanced her laundry basket and opened the door to her mother-in-law, Carmen. "Your wool suit looks snazzy on you. Is it new?"

"Yes, you can't work too hard at remaining attractive for your husband. Mine likes to see me in something new." Carmen put her purse down and eyed Choly critically. "You could use something new yourself. You can't make Jose proud when you wear dowdy things like this." Carmen fingered Choly's sweatshirt.

"All the money seems to go to our boys who are growing faster than our clothing budget." Choly resisted irritation.

"Look at this faded nightgown." Carmen picked

the offending garment from the top of the laundry basket. "How can Jose keep a spark when you wear dumpy bed clothes?"

Choly gave her irritation free reign.

❖ Stephanie ❖

"This tastes like hay. It must be good for us." Emily's brother-in-law grimaced as he tasted the appetizer Emily placed on the coffee table." His laugh didn't reduce the sting.

"Bet we get that weird carob stuff for desert," the other brother-in-law joined in the ribbing. "What else would you expect from a health food kook?"

"You boys stop," Stephanie, Emily's mother-in-law, scolded. "This is delicious food. Emily's good nutrition habits will have her running races when you're crippled old men." Stephanie swatted at her sons. "I tried to teach them manners," she apologized to Emily. "Obviously, they aren't displeased with the taste. Look at how much they've gobbled."

Seeing the hurt still on Emily's face, she put her arm around her. "Let's go in the kitchen and see if I can help you finish getting dinner, while these baboons chomp on the hors d'oeuvres."

In the kitchen Stephanie took Emily's hands and quietly prayed for the hurt feelings. Warmly, Emily hugged her.

The Tongue Is a Little Member

"Consider what a great forest is set on fire by a small

spark. The tongue also is a fire, a world of evil among the parts of the body. It corrupts the whole person, sets the whole course of his life on fire,...but no man can tame the tongue. It is a restless evil, full of deadly poison" (James 3:5b-6b,8).

More than any other factor, our tongue determines how we are perceived as a mother-in-law. Powerful, it gets us into or out of trouble. No matter how much we'd like, we can't suck our words back once they're uttered. We're stuck with their effect. We want our words to effect good. An intriguing physics idea purports that sound never dies; it simply circulates around in the air forever. In the same way our words hastily spoken can circulate around the mind in endless reruns for good or for bad. Some in-law jokes stem from bad reruns. One says, "Do you know what a mother-in-law sandwich is? Cold shoulder and raw tongue." Our tongue has the power to either hurt and offend our in-laws or to make them feel loved and accepted. Deuteronomy 18:10a says, "Let no one be found among you who sacrifices his son or daughter in the fire." Without thinking we can say words that have the effect of fire on the emotions of our family. In dissension, arguments, or torn loyalties, our family suffers as if passing through the fire.

Prayer brings protection from harming our relationships with our tongue. Before phoning, visiting, speaking about sensitive subjects, or in tense situations, PRAY. If we invite God, He can supply us with words of grace or stop us from speaking entirely. "A man finds joy in giving an apt reply—and how good is a timely word!" (Proverbs 15:23).

Use Our Tongue

For Praise

Take a tip from the apostle Paul. He always began his letters with praise. Later he sometimes took his readers to task, but he praised what was right and good first. Be generous with praise. It doesn't cost anything and buys an abundance of good will. Praise often. Praise small, insignificant things as well as big, important things.

Determine we will speak only good of our in-laws. "Finally, brothers, whatever is true, whatever is noble, whatever is right, whatever is pure, whatever is lovely, whatever is admirable—if anything is excellent or praiseworthy—think about such things" (Philippians 4:8). If we think hard enough we can find virtues in our in-laws. But they won't know we have until we go beyond thinking them to speaking them.

Everyone has *some* good qualities—if it's only pretty cuticles. Talk about what's good. For the not so good, use our tongue to pray instead.

Praise good money sense, a good decision, housekeeping, or whatever aspect of it you can praise. Every cook likes to have her dishes praised. The highest form of praise for cooking is asking for the recipe.

When praise spoken to a third party finally gets back to the complimented person's ears, it means even more than something good said to our face. Be sure our comments to others are the kind we'd want repeated.

When we praise our family, we set an example for

them to follow and hope they, also, will speak well of us. "Do to others as you would have them do to you" (Luke 6:31).

Praise helps the in-law love us and love helps us let down our guard. When we no longer need to feel guarded, we move past the superficial to more depth of communication and relationship.

On the other hand, don't require our in-laws to bolster our emotional infrastructure with compliments. People avoid those who always need their self-esteem reinforced. Bolstering someone becomes a burden that squelches a relationship. Comments enhancing our sense of self-worth need to come voluntarily from the younger generation. When people weary of making us feel okay about ourselves, they avoid us.

For Kindness

"She openeth her mouth with wisdom; and in her tongue is the law of kindness" (Proverbs 31:26 KJV). It pleases the Lord when we show kindness. When we hear criticism of someone, we can deflect it by pointing out good qualities in the person being criticized. Instead of joining criticism, we speak about what underlies the attitude or action being criticized, enlarging our hearer's understanding of the person criticized.

My mother is a master at this skill. "But," she adds when hearing an unkind comment, "they probably feel unsure about themselves." The family quickly gets into a positive tone around her.

For Apology

"If you have been trapped by what you said, ensnared by the words of your mouth, then do this, my son, to free yourself . . . Go and humble yourself . . ." (Proverbs 6:2-3). Be quick to apologize if we sense we have offended. Whether we are right or wrong is not important. An apology quickly spoken prevents a small offense from growing large. We sow what we reap. Apologies produce a good crop. If we catch ourselves taking sides, arguing, or criticizing, an immediate apology helps clear the weeds.

Don't Use Our Tongues

For Criticism

✧ Nora ✧

"Your neighbor's real friendly," Nora said, setting the empty laundry basket on the floor and shutting the door of her daughter-in-law's kitchen. "She told me she can always tell when I'm visiting, because the laundry's so much brighter."

✧ Marie ✧

"Miles, could you help me carry my picnic basket?" Miles's mother, Marie, stepped out of her car at the park.

"It's heavy." Miles hoisted his mother's basket onto the picnic table beside the basket of food his wife had packed for the occasion.

Marie looked at her daughter-in-law and said, "I brought a lot so Miles would have something he likes to eat."

Criticism tears the fabric of relationships, and it accomplishes little. As in-laws, we aren't character developers. What we say with our tongue will not change them, but our quiet example might. Criticism breeds distrust and defensiveness. Frankness in the guise of truthfulness leaves wounds.

Also avoid criticizing the in-law's family. Although we may grumble about our own family, no one likes an outsider criticizing their family members. When our in-laws complain about their family, we'd better hush. We can rise to the defense of our child's spouse without participating in running down the family.

✧ *Sherry* ✧

"Don't tell your son what to do," Sherry said, "even if you think your prodding is helping me. If you nag him, I'll probably get less help. We're satisfied about the way our home operates. Be happy we are happy, and be quiet." Sherry felt better after spilling her feelings.

Her mother-in-law swallowed hard and apologized.

Sometimes the sacrifices of motherhood are the sacrifices of silence. If we expect God to do the changing, we won't resort to our tongue to effect change. "My soul, wait thou only upon God; for my expectation is from him" (Psalm 62:5 KJV).

For Unsought Advice

✧ *Anita* ✧
"One more game, Grandma," Sammy wheedled.

"Grandma is tired, Sammy, and you'll feel tired tomorrow in school if you stay up later," Sammy's mother answered for Anita, his grandmother. "Put the game away and go to bed."

"One TV program first, Momma, then I'll go to bed," Sammy whined. His parents sighed.

Five days into her visit, Sammy's grandmother, Anita, was not surprised Sammy watched one TV show. Indeed, he stayed up for one more program and then one more after that. Bedtime on school nights wasn't early in this household. Instead of offering advice, at her own bedtime, Anita prayed. She asked the Lord to help Sammy get the rest he needed to remain alert in school.

The day she left for home, a note arrived from school stating that Sammy often seemed lethargic at school, and would his parents please see to it he went to bed earlier. Anita managed to suppress the grin wanting to sweep over her face at the answer to prayer.

If they don't ask for advice, don't volunteer it. Worry provides the impulse to give unrequested advice. Verbalizing our worry gives the impression we question their knowledge or wisdom to manage their lives.

A by-product of unsought advice is guilt. We moms are famous for producing colossal guilt trips for our grown children. There's a daily comic strip, *Momma*, which devotes a large percentage of its column to that topic.

The more often we offer advice the kids don't want, the less they are apt to hear, heed or follow it. Resistance builds, not compliance. One mother said, "When I open my mouth, they close their ears."

✧ *Mary Beth* ✧

"I have the most wonderful mother-in-law," Mary Beth spoke with affection. *"She absolutely trusts us to make the right decisions and to do the right thing. She always has, even when we were first married. Of course, our choices weren't always good, but you would never know from listening to her."*

It would be a boring world if everyone decorated just like us, cooked the same way, or cleaned house to the same degree. Even children within the same family require a variety of procedures. Each generation will approach life differently.

Once again, prayer is the best antidote for the urge to advise. Placing our concerns in the hands of God helps us keep our noses out of their business. When our children were home, their activities were our business—not any more. They need space to develop discernment. Discernment requires exercise to develop.

One question on my form was, "What do you most appreciate about your mother-in-law?" "She doesn't interfere," was a frequent answer. Advice that is unsought is interpreted as interfering. When the advice was requested, people expressed appreciation for it.

"I can handle a concern presented so there is no doubt the decision is mine," Earl said. "If I know my mother-in-law will stay out of it after speaking her concern, that's fine." His wise mother-in-law limited her verbalized concerns to a very few. Many young women, however, liked their mother-in-law sharing recipes, household hints, even tips on handling children when the young wife opened the subject first. It's a fine line we mothers-in-law walk.

For Arguing

"Starting a quarrel is like breaching a dam; so drop the matter before a dispute breaks out" (Proverbs 17:14).

If a subject comes up and we suspect our thoughts are contrary to our in-law's opinion, we can opt to remain quiet. The problem comes when we *don't* realize we are treading dangerously. A quick change of subject can rescue us. A handy reservoir of such phrases as these can smooth over the scene: "You may be right;" "I hadn't looked at it like that before;" and "I respect your point of view."

Arguments between the couple are also awkward. When trapped as bystanders witnessing an argument between our young couple, find comfort in the flattering fact they feel relaxed enough around us to argue. Go wash the dishes, read a magazine, or otherwise KEEP OUT OF IT. "Like one who seizes a dog by the ears is a passer-by who meddles in a quarrel not his own" (Proverbs 26:17). Moms don't take sides. Sticking up for our child doesn't help. Smiling does, even if it does appear somewhat frozen.

"A gentle answer turns away wrath, but a harsh word stirs up anger" (Proverbs 15:1). When a disagreement boils, don't assume the role of go-between. Go-betweens get smashed in the middle. After a while, we will become skilled at what subjects to avoid with our new family member.

For Complaining

"Do everything without complaining or arguing," (Philippians 2:14). "I complained, and my spirit was overwhelmed. Selah" (Psalm 77:3b KJV).

Complaining also overwhelms the listener's spirit. People do not crave the companionship of complainers. Enough said. Let's set the example of dwelling on the uplifting aspects of life. Our tone of voice can contribute to the interpretation that we are complaining. Let's leave whining to childhood.

For Boring Them

Ecclesiastes 3:7 says there is "a time to be silent and a time to speak." Be careful to allow others to talk. Don't be afraid of silence. Several questionnaires mentioned nonstop talking on the part of the mother-in-law as an irritant. Much chatter stems from nervousness.

"Do not be quick with your mouth, do not be hasty in your heart to utter anything before God. God is in heaven and you are on earth, so let your words be few" (Ecclesiastes 5:2). Good advice.

Several questionnaires mentioned a mother-in-law who talked "incessantly." Usually if we are interested in the conversation, we do not consider the talking to be incessant. We can tell if we are talking about topics that interest our in-laws if we watch their faces and bodies. Glassy-eyed stares and rote polite responses provide clues to change the subject, or better yet, turn the floor over to them. If they're enthusiastic, we can continue. When dealing with the younger generation, allow them to steer the direction of the conversation. Find out their interests and discuss them.

Listen well. Listening is an indispensable contribution to conversation. Listen at least as much as we talk. "When words are many, sin is not absent, but he who holds his tongue is wise" (Proverbs 10:19).

Our tongue establishes the heart and depth of any relationship. By using the same conversational graces for our family that we use with outsiders, we make a climate for love to grow. What we learn from controlling our tongue with our in-laws will create the added blessing of enhancing our relationship with everyone else.

❖ Use the tongue for frequent praise.
❖ Use the tongue to apologize readily.
❖ Refrain from:
   criticism,
   unsought advice,
   arguing,
   complaining,
   boring.

✧ *Six* ✧

Going Easy on Mistakes

✧ **Bonnie and Pam** ✧

"What can I do to help with the dinner?" Pam smiled at her daughter-in-law as she walked into the kitchen.

"Would you please peel the potatoes?" Bonnie asked, handing her mother-in-law the peeler and motioning toward the potatoes next to the sink.

"Where do you want the peelings?" Pam asked, motioning toward the sink and trying not to wrinkle her nose at the rancid odor rising from a mess she could not identify in the sink.

"Not there," Bonnie said offering her a piece of newspaper. "Those are the scraps I've been collecting to feed the dog."

"Oh." Since Pam couldn't think of a safe comment, she applied her attention to the potatoes *while Bonnie scraped the offending scraps out of the sink and deposited them in a bowl for the dog. After setting the dish on the step for Fido, Bonnie took out a package of fresh chicken from the refrigerator, unwrapped it and dumped it into the sink where the scraps had rested.*

Pam felt her stomach churn into her throat. Probably just as well, she thought. Keeps me from opening my mouth and saying anything. Hope cooking the chicken takes care of any bacteria it picks up from the filthy sink. Silently she prayed for the Lord to help Bonnie learn sanitary practices and to protect all their stomachs in the meantime.

✧ **Paula and Ruth Ann** ✧

"Joey, stop getting under my feet. Go somewhere else to play." Paula's voice was shrill as she un-ceremoniously gave Joey a little push in the direction of the door.

Ruth Ann kept her eyes glued to the biscuit dough she rolled out in her daughter-in-law's kitchen.

Paula, ashamed of her outburst, moved into the dining room to lay out the silverware.

"The sun shining on your golden hair almost makes it look as if you have a halo."

Paula looked up surprised.

Ruth Ann stood in the doorway. "A halo's ap-propriate, you know. You're an angel in my eyes. I love to hear you pray, to hear what the Lord shows you in the Bible."

"How can you say that when I was so cross just

now and pushed Joey aside?"

"I didn't say you're always angelic. Thank goodness, you're human. Keeps you from being impatient with my failings." Both women laughed. "Hug Joey and make it right. I still think you're like an angel. I'm glad you make time for God."

Glowing from the compliment, Paula proceeded to confess impatience with her toddler. She listened attentively to Ruth Ann's suggestions.

Every day our children make choices—from mundane things like food selection, quantity of food consumed, and housekeeping patterns, to the more important issues like use of money, approach to child rearing, application of Christian beliefs and methods of dealing with quarrels. Choices carry consequences. We fear the possibility their wrong choices might cause disaster.

In this chapter, we will not consider those grave choices that result in life-shaking dangerous consequences discussed in chapter 11. Here we will investigate our attitude toward our young couple's everyday human mistakes.

Good Judgment Develops

Good judgment doesn't spring up suddenly. It develops as we mature. Slipping wedding rings on their fingers at the altar doesn't cause the ability to make wise choices to slide onto the couple's personalities. Relationship skills don't come prepackaged, ready to break open at marriage. Skills and judgment develop. While these skills mature we muster up forbearance. *Webster's Seventh New Collegiate Dictionary* gives the definition of forbearance as refraining from the enforcement of something that is due. For the word forborne, the definition reads: "to bear with, endure, to leave alone, be patient." Patience is a good mother-in-law trait.

"But the wisdom that comes from heaven is first of all pure; then peace-loving, considerate, submissive, full of mercy and good fruit, impartial and sincere" (James 3:17). "Blessed is he whose transgressions are forgiven, whose sins are covered" (Psalm 32:1). By covering our children's mistakes we bless them. When a mistake is covered, it is not discussed. "Hatred stirs up dissension, but love covers over all wrongs" (Proverbs 10:12). Our love and wisdom allow us to apply the dictionary definitions above to our children's mistakes.

Whose Mistake Is It?

The mistake belongs to the one who makes it. Therefore the correction of the mistake belongs to the same person. If we didn't make the mistake, we're not responsible to straighten it out. Pointing out mistakes isn't a mother-in-law's role. We are called to love. Love covers mistakes. "[Love] rejoiceth not in iniquity, ...beareth all things, believeth all things, hopeth all things, endureth all things" (1 Corinthians 13:6-7 KJV). Sounds like our forbearance definition, doesn't it? Since we love God, we believe He can influence our family into what He wants. The peace resulting from our belief in God's leading allows us to overlook negative situations and behavior.

It's God's responsibility, not ours, to straighten out our in-laws' thinking or their messes. "For the battle is not yours, but God's" (2 Chronicles 20:15c). It's comforting to know He fights a victorious war. "The voice of the LORD breaks the cedars; . . . The voice of the LORD shakes the desert;" (Psalm 29:5a, 8a). God's voice can speak to our adult children's mistakes better than our voice and not cause resentments.

✧ *Tom and May* ✧

"Why weren't you in church Sunday?" May asked her son-in-law.

"We were tired, Mother," Tom answered.

"It's a good thing God doesn't tire of you as easily as you get too tired for the Lord," May said. "If your Saturday night makes you want to sleep instead of going to church Sunday, you should change your Saturday plans."

In my survey, Tom admitted May was right. However, he didn't shift his priorities because of his mother-in-law's instruction. Much later, events in his life changed him, and he put God first.

Because we know ignoring God's ways ultimately brings grief, we long to speak about the mistakes we see. But unless God anoints the words and the proper moment to speak them, it is better to trust in the tender mercies of the Lord toward our adult children and pray. "The prayer of a righteous man [or mother-in-law] is powerful and effective" (James 5:16b). Our loving relationship may cause our in-laws to ask our opinion; otherwise, we withhold comment.

The Kids Are God's Pottery

"For those God foreknew he also predestined to be conformed to the likeness of his Son" (Romans 8:29a). God's plan for us and our children is the same, to conform us to the image of Jesus Christ, to make us Christlike. To accomplish this goal, our lives are dotted with trials, tests and blessings that mold us and prepare us for the roles God wants us to perform. "And the God of all grace, who called you to his eternal glory in Christ, after you have suffered a little while, will himself restore you and make you strong, firm and steadfast" (1 Peter 5:10). Remembering that God is interested in creating mature Christians that are trustworthy for His service, helps us become supportive and not critical when our children stumble and make mistakes. If we are to maintain our equilibrium while our children are on the Potter's wheel, we must develop ways to endure their trials just as we must develop ways to endure our own. Trials are as much a part of life as breathing. Our job is to figure how to endure and grow, and not fall apart in them.

Remember how our stomach knotted when a child ran into the house with a gash in his knee? We gritted our teeth and cleaned the wound, cringing with each pathetic wail. We learned not to overreact to the mishap. We minimized the damage and applied antiseptic.

Now with grown children, we cover the mistake with a bandage by not addressing it unless invited. We can put healing balm on the mistake by praying for God to right the error and show them the way He wants them to go. "Show me your ways, O LORD, teach me your paths" (Psalm 25:4).

Knowing our children have learned how to hear from God and obey what they hear is a source of peace for our old age. If they always hear first from us, how will they learn to sense and understand what God is speaking to their own hearts? They need to hear what He wants for their own choices and decisions. For them to develop strong spiritual muscles, they need the opportunity to exercise their spiritual muscles. Our silence gives them opportunity to exercise.

Show Mercy

"I don't appreciate being judged," Gwen wrote on her form. "Maybe I am a baby about some things, but then I'm still learning and I wish my mother-in-law understood that."

Lana wrote, "I fell and cut my knee while we were on a family hike. My mother-in-law ridiculed my tears. She sneered the rest of the walk, saying I magnified a little cut by limping," continued Lana. "I wanted her sympathy not her judgment. I think she only loves me when I meet her standards."

"A gracious *and* good woman wins honor" (Proverbs 11:16a, Amplified). "The merciful, kind *and* generous man *(or mother-in-law)* benefits himself [for his deeds return to bless him]" (Proverbs 11:17a, Amplified). Remembering our own youth increases our mercy. Remember the burned food, the thrown out dishes of fuzzy leftovers, the blouse purchased never to be worn, the feud over something trivial? Remember the time wasted, the ill-advised opinions, the black-and-white viewpoint, allowing little room for compromise? With time, God changed us and brought maturity.

"He also said, 'This is what the kingdom of God is like. A man scatters seed on the ground. Night and day, whether he sleeps or gets up, the seed sprouts and grows, though he does not know how. All by itself the soil produces grain—first the stalk, then the head, then the full kernel in the head'" (Mark 4:26-28). God changes the seed of grain into a full head of grain gradually. He will do the same for our family. He will change us into His image gradually. He will change others gradually. We can focus on what's good and ignore the unfinished parts of others' personalities. We postpone judgment while our loving Father is molding them. Grateful for our quiet mercy, our children will love and appreciate us. In return, they become more willing to tolerate our weaknesses. Mercy makes our time together more pleasant and, thus, more desired.

Finally, we remember we probably don't have the final word on what's right and what constitutes a mistake, anyway. What is right for one family is not always right for another.

Shake off Guilt

The most painful aspect of seeing our grown children make mistakes comes if we realize we con- tributed, in part at least, to their unfortunate attitude, point of view, or philosophy. Being imperfect, it is unlikely we raised perfect kids. "For all have sinned and fall short of the glory of God" (Romans 3:23).

When we recognize our contribution to some problem, our first step is to repent to God. Pray about the matter and ask if God wants us to apologize to our child. There are times when we remain silent in order not to convey disapproval to the grown child. But if God directs, spoken repentance brings healing. The younger generation knows we aren't perfect and appreciates knowing we also recognize our imperfections.

Next, forget. Don't allow the enemy of our soul to drag the old matter back up and use it to wash us in guilt. Don't allow it's memory to cause us to despair for the future of the grown children. Go forward, refusing to rehash the mistake in our thinking or conversation. Once we repent, the matter is finished.

"Then he adds: 'Their sins and lawless acts I will remember no more' " (Hebrews 10:17). If God doesn't remember, we don't need to either. Guilt enlarges our fear that our children will make mistakes. Ridding ourselves of guilt eliminates a key reason we succumb to lecturing our children and their spouses about their faults. Refuse to let the comments or insinuations of others bathe us in guilt. Don't worry about what others are thinking. People are often too self-centered to give us much thought, anyway. The Lord knows where we've failed and where we are innocent. He's capable of protecting our reputations. Besides, if people realize we have failings, they are more apt to relate to us and listen when we talk about Jesus.

Our Reward

"Her children arise and call her blessed" (Proverbs 31:28a). We all hope our children will want to follow this verse. It's more likely to happen if we don't rub their noses in their failings. On my survey, a frequently repeated answer to the question about the qualities people liked best in their mothers-in-law was: "She doesn't interfere and minds her own business." We can share our own mistakes and hope they learn from them, but the application to their own lives must be theirs. We can't force the parallel.

Our children will make mistakes. Our relationship will profit from overlooking these mistakes. As a result of overlooking them, our children are more apt to listen to our bits of wisdom. Forgiveness is a cornerstone for good in-law relationships. Our in-law's mistakes give us opportunity to practice forgiveness.

By developing ourselves, as discussed in the next chapter, we will have less time for preoccupation with our adult children's mistakes. When confronted with a mistake, remember the following things: God sees, cares, and is not surprised. We certainly make our own share of mistakes. It seems mistakes are part of the human condition.

- ✧ Be patient while we wait for God to develop maturity in others.
- ✧ Pray for their failings; focus on their strengths.
- ✧ Remember God is the best corrector.
- ✧ Repent of our failings; then forget them.

✧ *Seven* ✧

Developing Myself

✧ **Addie** ✧

"Mom, we're having Tyrone's five-year-old birthday party Saturday and want you and Dad to come. Can you shake free from your painting around 2:00 to celebrate with us?"

"Of course, I'll squeeze it in somehow. Wouldn't miss his big day for anything." When Addie hung up the phone she shook her head in wonderment. "What a different life I have now," she remarked.

"Three years ago, you'd have been worrying about why you hadn't been called for a party yet, on the phone begging to be included in the party and fretting about the details," Addie's husband laughed.

"I'll have to work extra hard to finish those commissioned flower paintings before Tyrone's party."

85

"Aren't you glad you took art lessons?"

"And to think I never thought I had any talent."

"I'm proud of you, hon. You're more fun to live with, too." Lamar ducked as Addie pretended to aim a fist at him. They both grinned.

✧ *Julie* ✧

The sound of the phone startled Julie. Her knees creaked from kneeling on the floor when she arose to answer it.

"Mother Julie, I'm sorry to call when I know it's your prayer time, but I'm so worried. I thought you could add my mother to your prayers today. The doctor looked so sober when he told us about the tests he wanted to run. We both got scared."

"I've been praying for her ever since you told me about her symptoms, dear. Dad and I are praying. God isn't surprised by the problem. He has the whole matter under control. I hope knowing people are praying helps."

"Thanks, Mother Julie, you always make me feel better. I'm so glad you're a praying mother-in-law. I wish I was as disciplined in my prayer life as you are."

New Directions

When a child marries, a large responsibility is removed from our life, not the socializing and involvement with our child, but the responsibility. This frees chunks of time and emotional energy for other pursuits. What have you always wanted to do but never had time for? What have you always wanted to try, but avoided because you thought you'd fail? Look at Addie. She lived a quiet life never suspecting her outstanding ability to paint flowers. The skill she developed led her to a fulfilling and profitable pursuit.

New interests create fresh excitement for our lives. Launch out and experiment with new activities, hobbies, or a self-improvement project after a child marries. Such pursuits help us gracefully take a back seat in the lives of our married children. With our children grown, we trade the end of a phase we treasured for new adventure.

Possible New Horizons

Spiritual Development

"They devoted themselves to the apostles' teaching and to the fellowship, to the breaking of bread and to prayer" (Acts 2:42). Greg and Shelly left their jobs and community to go to China as missionaries when their last child left home. The experience broadened the horizons of the entire extended family. What could you do to expand your spiritual muscles? Attend a Bible study class you couldn't fit in before. Open up your house to a Bible study or prayer group. Enlarge your personal devotion time. Spend time with other Christians and those you hope will become Christians.

We can't use time any better than pursuing what Paul prays for Christians in Ephesians 1:17-18: "I keep asking that the God of our Lord Jesus Christ, the glorious Father, may give you the Spirit of wisdom and revelation, so that you may know him better. I pray also that the eyes of your heart may be enlightened in order that you may know the hope to which he has called you, the riches of his glorious inheritance in the saints."

Like Julie in the story at the beginning of the chapter, we will serve as a good example to our family and build up treasure in heaven while we accomplish God's tasks for us on earth. Deuteronomy 4:40 tells us we should keep God's commandments so that it will go well with us and our children after us. What better motivation to learn more about the commandments and the Commander. While growing in knowledge of His faithfulness and goodness, we become better equipped for the trials of life and better able to help others with their difficulties.

"She's a woman of prayer." On my questionnaire, people cited this attribute frequently as the most appreciated characteristic of a mother-in-law. With our children out of the house, we have plenty of opportunities to spend uninterrupted blocks of time communing with God.

Romance

✧ *Corine and Gil* ✧

*"You never pay any attention to me. You're reading the newspaper while I'm trying to talk to you."
Exasperated, Corine pushed the top of the paper down to peer at Gil.*

"I'm sorry," Gil answered, looking at her. "What were you saying?"

"I'm saying our marriage needs a new spark. I need to feel important to you."

"How's this?" Gil flung the paper aside and

grabbed Corine in a rib-crushing hug.

Corine smiled. "Great, but I can't make one hug last a week."

"Let's make a pact. Every time we pass each other, we'll stop at least for a pat or a hug," Gil suggested.

"When we were first married, we couldn't keep our hands off each other," Corine remembered. "I read if you act like what you want to feel, the feelings will follow the action. Let's act like newly-weds, dippy crazy over each other."

To their delight, it worked. By reminding each other, Corine and Gil put frequent, affectionate touching back into their marriage and found that new love and appreciation blossomed.

"Let him kiss me with the kisses of his mouth—for your love is more delightful than wine" (Song of Songs 1:2). I know this book of the Bible contains symbolism for Jesus Christ, but let's apply it to us here. Remember when you longed for a little more privacy, less interruptions from the children? Take advantage of less interruptions now. Marriage requires revitalization. In the urgency of child rearing, sometimes the nurturing of our marriage gets slap dash attention. Now is our chance to change that.

Thrill your husband by giving him a dose of ranking first place in your life. Read a book aloud together. Take an interest in his hobbies—you did when you dated, remember? Search out the free or inexpensive recreation in your area and arrange regular dates together. Cook dishes he especially enjoys eating.

Take a second honeymoon. Use the money liberated by having one less person living in your house.

Do you have a habit that irritates your husband? Give him a present by working to eliminate it. Have you accumulated some areas of friction over the years? Pull them out in the open and reduce them. Seek counseling if you need it. With the years of child rearing over, our reward is time to savor each other. Make the marriage a top priority.

Friendships

✦ *Jean and Lynn* ✦

Jean hummed while she dialed her friend's phone number. "Lynn, there's a special string en-semble playing Thursday night. Let's go; and, afterwards, we'll get a snack and have a good chat," Jean spoke into the phone. After a long pause, she asked, "Lynn, are you there?"

"Yeah, I'm here," Lynn answered. "Look, maybe I'll see you there, but Clara already arranged to go with me. Sorry. We do need to get together for a chat. Maybe next week."

"Okay," Jean allowed her voice to grow flat. "Bye, now."

"I wish Jean had more friends," Lynn sighed as she hung up the phone. "She always seems of-fended if I do something without her."

Friendships are especially important for single mothers. Without friends there is a temptation for us to look to the children for all our fulfillment and recreation. When the children are the only other breathing bodies in your house, their leaving results in a hollow-sounding home. Plenty of other lonely women are eager to share friendship with you. Seek them out.

"A friend loves at all times" (Proverbs 17:17a). Friendships are like flowers in our lives. They refresh our spirits and beautify our lives. Cultivate them with diligence and persistence. Like any garden, they need care. They die from neglect and require regular feeding. Be careful to avoid the pesticides of neglect and criticism.

Time and effort are required to make sure of our friends. Proverbs 27:10 says, "Do not forsake your friend and the friend of your father, . . . better a neighbor nearby than a brother far away." With our child married, there's more time available for fellowship. Develop many friends so we don't suffocate anyone by requiring too much of our friendship as Jean did.

Friends can come from all age groups. Become a mother to young girls who live away from family. Adopt a grandmotherly role toward some handy children. While you gain, they do also. In our mobile society, many young women live too far away to enjoy much contact with their mothers. Since the older generation supplies an important balance to the clamor of new ideas in today's world, the opportunity for companionship with an older Christian woman offers the younger one strength and motivation to uphold Biblical principles.

Service to Others

"She opens her arms to the poor and extends her

hands to the needy" (Proverbs 31:20). One group of women joined their talents and energies to provide the girls of their church with free wedding reception help. They decorate the reception hall, help plan a menu, prepare the food, and keep the platters full. Occasionally, they also orchestrate wedding rehearsal dinners, complete with "waiters" wearing black coats and carrying towels over their arms. The "waiters," actually the women's husbands, are busy professional men serving God's people. A lovely wedding is within reach of all the brides of their church for a small cost. Plus, the women reap joy with buckets of love and gratefulness poured in their direction. These women win a permanent place of love in many hearts.

Develop Skills and Hobbies

Do you like to read? Broadening the range of books you read will give your conversation skills a sparkle. Take lessons: art, music, golf, swimming. In her fifties, my mother learned to swim after I married. It was a source of satisfaction to her to conquer water after all those years. Go back to school. Launch a new career.

Daughters-in-law frequently praised mothers-in-law for sewing gifts. With gratitude, woman after woman mentioned clothing made for themselves or their children by the mother-in-law. One woman remembered World War II when material was scarce and money was tight. Her mother-in-law made skirts for her granddaughters out of the legs cut off of old trousers. After all these years, those gifts are still remembered and appreciated.

Take an aerobics class. Begin regular walking. Exercise does wonders for our emotional outlook. Articles abound telling us mystifying reasons for this; but, whatever the reason, we cheer ourselves with exercise.

Record Family History

Many people expressed gratitude for their mother-in-law filling them in on family history. Some did it in conversations. Some wrote family stories down. Others spoke them into a tape recorder. One mother enjoyed the year she collected pictures and letters from all the scattered branches of the family through two generations and made them into a scrapbook as a gift for the oldest family member. Although not her original intention, it became a treasured heirloom for future generations.

Personality Plus

"May the words of my mouth and the meditation of my heart be pleasing in your sight, O LORD, my Rock and my Redeemer" (Psalm 19:14). Now is the time when we should reevaluate ourselves. Are all the nooks and crannies of our hearts acceptable to God? If not, then it will be hard for all our words to be pleasing to God, whether we are praying or talking to others.

Thick Skin

Learning to relate to new in-laws offers a good time to bolster beneficial attitudes. One splendid attribute is a thick skin: not the one draped around our body, but the one covering our emotions. There is an element of choice in hurt feelings. We have the power to decide whether or not we will allow ourselves to feel hurt. We choose how often and how long we allow ourselves to mull over the words or actions that wounded us. When we don't offend easily, people relax and enjoy our company. Don't we feel on guard around people who are easily upset? We can't change them, but we can determine to overcome our own sensitivity.

Forgiveness

Forgiveness is a strong pillar for healthy happy families. Build a tall, wide column of forgiveness in our personalities. Use it often. Forgiveness grows easier with practice.

While we are forgiving, let's forgive ourselves. "Who can discern his errors? Forgive my hidden faults" (Psalm 19:12). Don't allow our past and current mistakes to keep us discouraged. Once we've repented, we shouldn't relive our mistakes in regret again and again. People tire of propping us up when we are down on ourselves. Learn from the mistake and go forward. One valuable result of mistakes is becoming more charitable in our judgment of others. We understand the vulnerability of humanity, so we should be more merciful.

While we're learning the art of relating to our children's spouses, take a moment to think about your own mother-in-law. Were there times when you failed to provide the grace and understanding she needed? Did you judge her harshly? If she no longer lives, go to God and ask for forgiveness. If you still have her, go to her. Express your appreciation of her. After assuming the role of mother-in-law, we understand its snares better than when we were you

Joy

Ask God for joy. People gravitate to upbeat pe
sonalities. Joy is one of God's character traits listed
in Galatians 5:22. If we are to be conformed to His
image we require a good strong dose of joy.
Cooperate in acquiring joy by refusing to dwell on
pessimistic thoughts. A robust sense of humor is a
grand quality. Ask God for it. It can't help but make
us more fun.

If we are having trouble feeling joyful, then start by
developing a thankful heart. Be thankful for the little
things. It pleases God and makes us pleasant to be
around. Thankfulness brings contentment which
leads to joy.

"He cuts off every branch in me that bears no fruit,
while every branch that does bear fruit he prunes so
that it will be even more fruitful" (John 15:2). A
pruning takes place in our family when our child
marries and leaves home. With proper treatment,
pruning causes good fruit. Our pruning can be the
beginning of new growth and a rich fruit crop as we
use our opportunities to develop ourselves.

- ✧ Deepen our spiritual life.
- ✧ Renew romance in our marriage.
- ✧ Cultivate friendships.
- ✧ Develop skills and hobbies.
- ✧ Research family history.
- ✧ Launch a personality improvement pro-
  gram.

✧ *Eight* ✧

The Special Needs of Daughters-in-Law

✧ **Natasha and Rosemary** ✧

Natasha smiled to herself as she left the grocery store with a carton of sour cream. It was worth the extra stop on her way home from work to pick it up. Jerome would love the new recipe she wanted to make for dinner tonight.

"Oh no!" Natasha groaned as she approached her driveway. Her mother-in-law's car was parked in front of the house. "Not again. Doesn't she think I cook good enough for her son?" Fuming, Natasha walked in and went straight to the kitchen.

"Hi, Natasha." Rosemary, her mother-in-law smiled at her from the steaming pot she stirred on the stove. "I nearly have dinner ready. Would you slice some lemon for the tea?"

"But I planned to fix stroganoff. The beef's already cut in strips in the refrigerator," Natasha protested.

"I found the beef. It's perfect for a delicious stew—just the way Jerome likes it."

"But this is our one-month wedding anniversary. I planned an intimate little celebration." Natasha didn't know whether to cry or rage at her foiled plans.

◇ Charlotte and Katie ◇

"What a beautiful grandson you gave me." Charlotte reached out to pat the blue bundle her daughter-in-law, Katie, held as she sat up in her hospital bed.

Katie smiled; but, almost imperceptibly, drew her newborn slightly away.

"When my first baby was born, I felt so protective about him," Charlotte commented. "I was uncomfortable when anyone except my mother held him. Somehow I knew my mother would do everything right, but I was nervous about anyone else. I'll understand if you find you feel that way."

Katie threw her head back laughing. "That's just how I feel. Here. Hold Brian. You've made me feel better already."

A Challenge

Common opinion holds it is more difficult to be the mother-in-law to our daughter-in-law than to our son-in-law. The reason is our roles in the home are subject to comparisons. Regardless of what a person may do outside the home, the duties we daily perform in the home are similar although they're performed differently from house to house. Therefore there are more areas where a mother-in-law and a daughter-in-law can directly compare and contrast their styles. The mother-in-law and son-in-law have different roles and functions in the family-reducing comparisons and competition.

Ways to Bless Daughters-In-Law

Give Son Over

The saying goes: A son's a son 'til he takes a wife. A daughter's a daughter all of her life. Because a man traditionally spends more hours working than at home each week, his free time for his parents is also his only free time for his wife. If we can gracefully accept this fact and understand his time demands, we will reduce our expectations of his time and energies and yield them to his wife.

"'For this reason a man will leave his father and mother and be united to his wife, and the two will become one flesh'" (Ephesians 5:31). Tell her in words so she knows you know this principle.

Pray for Her Daily

Since this woman is critically important to our son and our grandchildren's well being, strengthen her in every way possible. Over time, her judgment of us, the mother-in-law, will effect how our own son views us. Married, he's with his wife much more than his mother. She colors how he thinks of Mom. Ask the Lord to teach us how to pray for our daughter-in-law. In addition to enlisting God's control over our family, praying helps prevent us from keeping mental accounts of our daughter-in-law's sins of omission and commission. After praying, we leave it in the hands of God. Prayer is our best, first, and last recourse.

"Give therefore thy servant an understanding heart to judge thy people, that I may discern between good and bad: for who is able to judge this thy so great a people?" (I Kings 3:9, KJV). This is Solomon's plea as the king of a great nation. It's a good plea for the mother-in-law also. We need God to give us understanding of our family. When any quality alarms us, earnest prayer leads us to peace. God delights in using His power to benefit His people—even in-laws.

Women often mentioned how much they appreciated their mother-in-law praying for them and their children. Let her know you pray. Ask for her prayer requests.

Prevent Competition

✧ *Wendy* ✧

"Tell her no. Say we're busy," Wendy spoke through compressed lips. "She came last weekend."

Her husband hung up the phone. "It's too late; she's coming."

"She's been here 65 days already this year, and it's only October. I've kept a record on the calendar, so you'll see how much your mother comes. You'd think she'd get tired of that four-hour drive."

Let's not compete with our daughters-in-law for our son's affection or time, and let her make the chicken soup if he gets a cold.

It's useless and a waste of emotional energy for us to enter into competition with the generation following us. What a relief. We don't need to compete in hairdos, clothes, or energy.

If the mother-in-law possesses leadership qualities or enjoys unusual talent, be careful the daughter-in-law doesn't feel pressure to try to live up to the same. Deborah in Judges 4 wielded mighty power. Since she was married, she may have had children and, therefore, a daughter-in-law. If so, I imagine she used the good sense not to expect her daughter-in-law to follow in her footsteps.

Don't compete with our daughter-in-law's mother—either her role or her time. One gal wrote, "She can't be my mother. I already have one." Also allow our daughter-in-law time to develop friends in her own generation. Discourage comparisons with other daughters-in-law, or your son's old girlfriends. Stands to reason. Read on.

✧ *Erma and Maxine* ✧

"Give Di a call, Mark," Erma urged her son to call his old girlfriend. *"You can charge it to my phone bill if you call while you're here."*

"I don't think so," Mark answered. *His glance at his wife, Maxine, detected a glare in her eyes.*

"Come on. I have her number right here. She still carries a torch for you," Erma pressed Mark.

"No, Mom, I don't want to talk to Di," Mark said.

"She's a good girl. You shouldn't have dumped her."

Now there was no mistaking the smolder in Maxine's eyes.

Old girlfriends aren't even a good subject for teasing, let alone fostering contact.

Areas for Caution

Family Vacations

What a special treat it is for the entire family to go on a vacation together. It's important to insure the younger generation agrees with the idea. Family vacations involve careful planning. The younger generation needs to feel they have a choice about whether or not to participate, without the consequence of becoming the black sheep if they decline.

Probably the safest course is not to plan a vacation for the entire family every year. Poll the family for their views and wishes. Choose a facility which offers enough space for individual comfort. Make sure the financial arrangements for the vacation don't put any one family branch under too heavy a burden. Family vacations can foster deeper relationships through common fun while developing a collection of family jokes. Or they can become opportunities to grate on each other's nerves and to divide. Plan so no one individual feels he or she carries too much of the work load. Mom, stay on your toes to sense the needs of the in-laws.

Instruction

"Then they can train the younger women to love their husbands and children" (Titus 2:4). Verse 3 makes it plain this portion of scripture addresses the "older women" and closes with the words, "teach what is good."

Whoa! We can't rush out and design a seminar on wifely wisdom for our daughter-in-law. First in any relationship comes trust. Let's give her reason to trust us. By not judging her, by not talking behind her back, but by loving her and desiring the best for her, she'll come to trust us. Before we instruct our daughter-in-law, she must want to hear what we have to say. We can tell. She'll ask us. Until then, refrain from direct instruction and teach by the example of our own lives. Demonstration packs more power than words anyway.

Demonstrate forgiveness toward her where she needs it. It is just as important to demonstrate forgiveness in our conversation about others. A kind, charitable viewpoint toward others is one of the most valuable qualities we can possess. Give her, and others, credit for operating from good motivation, even when the results don't look too good.

Does our son have characteristics like his dad? Give his wife tips about how you handle them. Let her decide which tips she'll try. Tell her stories of her husband's youth. Wives treasure those. They add to her understanding of the man she married.

Instruction can go both directions. Several girls said they felt honored when their mother-in-law asked their opinions or advice about decisions or actions the mother-in-law was considering.

Appreciated Actions

Gail told me, "My mother-in-law realized it makes me nervous to have someone in the kitchen when I'm cooking. At meal preparation time, she takes the children outside or into another room and plays with them. It relieves a lot of tension for me." Be sensitive to the little hints daughters-in-law give about what they appreciate. Remember everyone is different. Just because we might like something doesn't mean they will.

Support

"My mother-in-law is special. She always puts us ahead of herself," Laura said. "She babysits for us, even on the spur-of-the-moment, when she's dead tired."

Over and over young couples listed babysitting as highly appreciated. Paying attention to the kids was high on the list. Some wrote they were grateful for in-laws who read stories, played games, and just plain talked with the children.

A number of women mentioned their mother-in-law looked after them or their children during a sickness, surgery, or accident. Anything done in the midst of an emergency carried indelible gratitude. Mothers moved in, came from out of state, dropped everything to rescue the situation—sometimes for long stretches.

Family Gatherings

A large gathering of strange people will intimidate newcomers. Whenever the larger extended family gathers for a reunion, wedding or funeral, remember your in-laws. Tuck them close to you and see they are introduced to everyone. Mention some tidbits about each person to make the person memorable and establish the relationship to the group. If possible, a rundown before the event will help keep all the relatives and friends straight. When the get-togethers are far apart, expect your in-law to forget some names and confuse relationships. After all, she hasn't the advantage of knowing them all her life as you have. Make sure she's not left alone or abandoned with the cousin who makes everyone uncomfortable.

When your young couple lives out of town and returns home for a visit, ask if they would like a gathering where they can see everyone at once instead of feeling they are running a marathon trying to visit everyone. While some might appreciate the abbreviated way to accomplish visiting, others may prefer the one-on-one conversations of smaller gatherings. Limit the urge to show off your prize-winning family if they have other plans for their visit.

A luncheon for a daughter-in-law and her special friends is a thoughtful gesture. Offering to babysit while she visits old friends is another good idea.

Gifts

✧ *Marjorie and Lindsay* ✧

"I'm closing my aunt's house so she can move into a nursing home. Would you like some of the antiques?" Marjorie asked her daughter-in-law, Lindsay.

"Shouldn't your daughters get them? After all, I'm just an in-law," Lindsay answered.

"You're family, too and I want you to have a chance to choose some of those lovely antiques, too."

One of the most repeated comments young ladies made in appreciation of their mothers-in-law was receiving the same treatment as their husband's sisters when gifts were given. The thoughtfulness of well-chosen gifts speaks acceptance. Of course, gifts are appreciated more if they are something the receiver really wants and can use. We moms should select the gifts to please our in-laws, rather than what we want them to have or to wear. Since strings attached to our gifts destroy their appreciation, don't expect to dictate the use of the gift. Neither should we give, expecting effusive thanks.

✧ *Ann and Bessie* ✧

Ann bit her tongue as she watched her neighbor unwrap the birthday gift that Ann's mother-in-law, Bessie, brought to the party. The tissue fell away revealing the picture Ann had laboriously cross stitched for Bessie's Mother's Day present only months before.

"So much for expending myself on her," Ann told me.

How do we receive the gifts our in-laws give us? With a strong show of genuine appreciation. One easy way to show gratitude is to actually use the item. Several girls expressed disappointment because their mothers-in-law never used their gifts. Receiving their gifts is one way to demonstrate we receive them.

The joys of a good relationship with a daughter-in-law are worth any effort. As our family enlarges with marriages and births, so does our opportunity for forgiving, loving, and serving.

- ✧ Allow our son to put his wife ahead of us.
- ✧ Pray for her daily.
- ✧ Discourage competition.
- ✧ Set an example of kindness and forgiveness.
- ✧ Get to know our daughter-in-law.
- ✧ Show consideration.

✧ ✑ine ✧

The Special Needs of
Sons-in-Law

✧ *Ed* ✧

Ed's suspicions flitted across his mind again. The nosiest mother-in-law on earth, he thought as he paused on his front porch before leaving for work. Changing his mind, he slipped the letter he had intended to post in the mail box into his pocket instead.

"I'll mail it from the office," he told his wife, kissing her goodbye. "That way your mother can't hold it up to the light and figure out how much our car payments are."

"Ed, that's not nice to say," Rene protested. "She's curious, but she's not a snoop."

"You think not? Let's run a test. I've been wondering about this every time she visits." Putting his

finger to his lips for silence and motioning to Rene to follow him, they stole up the staircase, carefully skipping the squeaking step. Reaching the top, he peered around the corner and motioned for Rene to look.

Just as they looked into their bedroom, Rene's mother flung back the top sheet of their bed and ran her hand over the bottom sheet. "I knew it," the woman muttered, leaning to inspect the sheet.

❖ *Sonia* ❖

"He's not God's best for you, Courtney." Sonia shook her finger at her daughter.

Courtney sighed. "Mother, I'm sick of your tirades about my husband. Sure, Dean's had some growing up to do, but he's changed a lot. Instead of griping about him, pray for him."

"I pray all right. I never miss a day praying about him. I pray everyday the Lord will remove Dean from your life."

Courtney and Sonia turned, startled by a sound. There stood Dean glowering in the kitchen door.

Give Respect
Focus on His Strengths

Ephesians 5:33 says, "the wife must respect her husband." Just as a woman needs love to blossom, a man needs respect. As mothers-in-law we help our daughters respect their husbands by conversing about the man's strengths, not pointing out his weaknesses. Since she lives with him, she's probably well aware of his faults and doesn't require any help in identifying them. Do her a favor and focus on his strengths.

Men may appear self-confident, totally in control on the outside, but hidden away in the heart of every man, as in every women, is a place that isn't self-sure. If we show our son-in-law respect, it reassures him of his worth—and he will love us for it.

"[Love] beareth all things, believeth all things, hopeth all things, endureth all things" (1 Corinthians 13:7 KJV) applies here as well as in chapter 5 when we discussed our tongue. Our belief in a person helps him become what we believe. People tend to live up to the expectations of those around them. Everyone craves approval, a wonderful present to give our sons-in-law.

Think of Gideon's mother-in-law. In Judges 6:11 Gideon, driven by fear of the Midianites, hid to thresh wheat. He said, "My clan is the weakest in Manasseh, and I am the least in my family" (Judges 6:15b). Do you think he impressed his mother-in-law? We don't know what she thought about her daughter's husband, but we can imagine her dumbfounded by the changes God brought to him and the boldness of the task God gave him, not to mention his astounding success. In a few short days, her fearful son-in-law became a national hero. Bet she never suspected the potential. What wonderful qualities and talents lie hidden in our sons-in-law? Ask God how to pray for these men. Expect to see the best God intends for them take place. We may be surprised and pleased.

Respect His Finances

❖ **Bryan and Bruce** ❖

Bryan said, "Whenever my mother-in-law comes to my house, she brings several bags of groceries to help with the expense of her visit. I appreciate her thoughtfulness and the treats she always includes."

Bruce said, "Whenever my mother-in-law comes to visit, she buys bags of groceries. Doesn't she think I feed my family good enough? I wish she wasn't so high and mighty and would eat what we serve."

We need to know if we are Bryan or Bruce's mother-in-law. It makes a difference how we behave. Same action, two responses. Taking the time to learn about our relative's feelings keeps us out of trouble.

❖ **Scott** ❖

"Mother took out a life insurance policy on me today," Vicki told her husband, Scott. "Wasn't that nice?"

"Why did she do that?" Scott asked.

"I'm not sure, but it's nice to know if I die, there's money."

"Who's the beneficiary?" Scott asked.

"Mother is," Vicki answered.

"Your mother took out insurance on you without saying a word to me. She made herself the beneficiary! Does she think I'm going to do you in or something?"

The realm of finances is touchy. What pleases one insults another. Exert caution not to compare the provision our sons-in-law supply with other family members. Ask God how to approach gift giving for them and their families—birthday, Christmas and in between. How much? How often? Will our gifts give them joy, create resentment, or interfere with the working of God in their lives? Several men told me their mothers-in-law lavished too many gifts on the kids. Others were grateful for the in-laws filling in with special treats their budgets could not afford. Find out what pleases your son-in-law. A man's ego is closely tied to his ability to provide for his family. Don't trample on him.

✧ *Yvonne and Karen* ✧

Karen and Mike were thrilled when Karen's mother, Yvonne, took them to the store to pick out a lovely bedroom suite.

"Not that one dear," Yvonne said when they looked at an inexpensive suite. "Find something nice. You'll live with it for years and years. Anyway I'm paying," Yvonne said and made a small down payment.

The week before the wedding, the store called to say they could not deliver the suite until completion of payment. Karen called her future mother-in-law.

"I can't afford it now, you'll just have to finish out the payment."

"But Mom, we didn't budget such a large amount of money."

"Be glad you're getting such a nice suite. You wouldn't have bought it if I hadn't given you a boost."

Although nearly every parent knows they should not, some parents use money to control. Resist pressuring them to spend beyond their means. Resist giving with strings attached. Pray to determine if our gift provides appreciated extras or makes the family feel we are critical of their lifestyle. Pray about giving when the kids have needs. Avoid destroying their sense of accomplishment.

✧ Rita and Ruth ✧

Carl asked his mother, Ruth, to go along to the ball game when he took his wife, Rita. Before the game they stood in line to buy popcorn. "I'd rather have a hot dog than popcorn," Rita grinned at Carl when they ordered.

Smiling, Carl forked over an extra dollar for Rita's wiener.

"You're extravagant. No wonder money's tight," Ruth reprimanded and swatted Rita with her umbrella.

Resist pressuring them for expenditures beyond their means. Also resist expressing judgment about how they spend their money.

The responsibility God places on men in the Bible is awesome. "If anyone does not provide for his relatives, and especially for his immediate family, he has denied the faith and is worse than an unbeliever"

(1 Timothy 5:8). The burden of providing for family in these times looms frighteningly large. If we have taught our daughter economical attitudes and approaches to her life style, we've made a good contribution. We mothers help by taking care not to plant ambitions or desires for expensive recreation, household items, or clothes. We resist making comparisons. We sow contentment in our conversations. By limiting our ambitions for our children to their closeness to God instead of clinging to material and recreational goals for them, we reduce our temptation to covet or push for a particular life style.

Respect His Privacy

Resist pumping our daughters for information beyond what the couple wants us to know. If we use our time with our daughter to delve into their affairs, our son-in-law will resent us and might even try to reduce our opportunities to be together. Don't pry!

Respect His Time

Don't encroach on his time with requests for chores you can manage some other way. Some men love to help; some love to but don't have time; some hate chores and barely manage the ones at their own house.

While respecting their time, recognize their need for recreation. Granted some men are selfish when making their time choices. They sacrifice their family when time is tight, scheduling golf or some other family-excluding activity. Let the couple work out their own solutions and compromises. We arouse stubbornness by entering the fray.

Whenever possible, use the time when he isn't home for our mother-to-daughter togetherness. That way we don't interfere with his plans, or infringe on their scarce time together. Also, we won't bore him when we talk girl stuff.

Respect His Authority in His Home

"For the husband is the head of the wife as Christ is the head of the church" (Ephesians 5:23a). As the head of his house, decisions belong to our son-in-law. We must leave the power of decision making in his hands, whether we agree or not. When our daughter and her husband differ on a decision, it's their job to reconcile their views. By honoring the man as the head of his house, we won't hinder their reaching mutual decisions they find satisfactory. We strive not to undermine the man married to our daughter knowing this can cause friction between them. Remember, we'll discuss the discouraging, disheartening situations in chapter 11.

He'll also appreciate us when we encourage our daughter to ask his advice before asking our advice, when we treat her as an adult who does not need her mother's say so on all matters. Better yet, treat him as an important family member by asking his advice.

What if he doesn't respect God or live a godly life? "The king's heart is in the hand of the LORD; he directs it like a watercourse wherever he pleases" (Proverbs 21:1). Our love and respect for what is good in his life can change him. It isn't likely our sermons will.

116

Ways to Bless a Son-In-Law

✧ *Peggy* ✧

"Slow down, Don; you have to turn in a few blocks. The interstate entrance is coming up," Peggy directed.

"I know Mom. I drive this way often," her son-in-law Don said, not taking his foot off the accelerator.

"Be careful; this is a dangerous intersection. Sometimes people barrel right through," Peggy said a block later. *"You'd better step on the brakes. Don't follow that car too close."*

"You'll drive the next time we take her somewhere," Don growled in a low voice to his wife.

Few men appreciate back seat directions. Read, embroider, do crossword puzzles, ask for an angel to accompany you and say nothing when your son-in-law drives.

Pray for Him

Our son-in-law carries the enormous weight of functioning as the spiritual head of his house. Remember, it takes time to grow into all our responsibilities. If his approach to his role leaves a lot to be desired, our best recourse is prayer. Nagging never created a spiritual growth spurt, but prayer changes things. Pray for his health, his job, his leadership in the home, his love for God, his devotional time, his relationship with his wife and children, and his disposition. Numbers of men said they were grateful for the daily

117

prayers of their mothers-in-law.

Show Interest in Him

When the men who filled out my questionnaire complained about their mother-in-law talking too much, I questioned them. The problem was her talk didn't interest them. Allow our son-in-law to guide the conversation in the direction of his interests. Take time to learn about his hobbies and ask intelligent questions. Take an interest in the sports he likes. Time spent to please another demonstrates genuine interest, especially in a world where time is precious.

"Let your conversation be always full of grace, seasoned with salt, so that you may know how to answer everyone" (Colossians 4:6). Some of the women in my survey expressed nervousness about conversing with their sons-in-law. If we ask God for His grace to come through us and His love to move through us for our son-in-law, we need not worry. Everyone responds to genuine love and acceptance.

"So Lot went out and spoke to his sons-in-law, who were pledged to marry his daughters. He said, 'Hurry and get out of this place, because the LORD is about to destroy the city!' But his sons-in-law thought he was joking" (Genesis 19:14). We don't know why Lot's sons-in-law responded this way; but, as a result of their response, they lost their lives and Lot's daughters lost their husbands. If we develop close relationships with our sons-in-law, we hope in times of crisis, they will listen and heed what we have to say. Remember all good relationships begin with true interest in the other person.

Show Appreciation

✧ *Todd* ✧

Todd loved woodworking. For his mother-in-law's Christmas gift, he selected the best wood he could afford to make a birdhouse for her. "It's a regular castle," he said wrapping it up. After failing to see it up in her yard all summer, he was furious to find it at her garage sale tagged $1.00.

"So much for pouring out my energies for my mother-in-law," he fumed.

✧ *Kent* ✧

Kent decided a picture frame was the perfect gift to make his mother-in-law for her birthday. She enjoyed displaying the pictures of her many grandchildren around her house. Proudly he gave it to her. While the pictures on display continued to multiply, his frame never appeared.

"I guess it hurt my feelings," he said.

✧ *Al* ✧

Al said, "Sometimes my mother-in-law sends me cards and notes telling me I am a good husband and father. That makes me feel good, because I know I'm not always."

We can't demonstrate too much gratitude for their gifts and favors. Don't take a good deed for granted; express and show appreciation.

Let's make ourselves the number one member of our son-in-law's fan club. The more we realize God's love and interest in our son-in-law, the easier it is to relax and concentrate on the man's strengths, leaving his weaknesses in God's hands and allowing respect for our daughter's husband to grow.

- ✧ Give him respect.
- ✧ Focus on his strengths.
- ✧ Accept his ability to provide.
- ✧ Respect his privacy.
- ✧ View him as the authority in his home.
- ✧ Pray for him.
- ✧ Show him interest and appreciation.

✧ *Ten* ✧

Influencing Grandchildren

✧ *Frances* ✧

"We're enjoying our grandchildren too much to bring them back to North Carolina yet," Frances spoke firmly into the phone.

"But, Mother," Trudy, her daughter-in-law, protested, "We only said you could take the children to New Jersey for a one-week visit. At 3 and 5, they're too young for long absences from Mom and Dad."

"They're both having a ball. Besides we don't have time now to drive down and bring them back," Frances answered.

"You've already had them three weeks. They don't sound fine to me; they sound homesick." By the time she hung up, Trudy was heartsick.

"I'm driving the car up to your folks and picking

up our kids whether you can go or not," Trudy announced to her husband. "You'd better find a ride if you have to stay here to work. Next weekend marks a month your folks have kept the children. That's too long for the first time they've left us. I'll never let them visit without us again."

✧ *Grace* ✧

"Hi, Mrs. Gorby," Cheryl greeted her neighbor as they pushed their grocery carts past each other down the cereal aisle.

"Look at your precious baby." Mrs. Gorby stopped to smile at Cheryl's infant who cooed from her baby seat propped up in the grocery cart. "She looked beautiful in her long white christening gown Sunday," Mrs. Gorby said. "She behaved beautifully, too. Never cried when the priest made the water cross on her forehead."

"You must have the wrong baby, Mrs. Gorby. We don't go to your church," Cheryl said.

"But Grace, your mother-in-law does," Mrs. Gorby innocently continued. "Of course, this is the baby she brought forward for baptism Sunday. You can't mistake those blonde curls."

"Well, Grace baby-sat this weekend while we were away for a wedding," Cheryl began to sputter. "But we've told her our church doesn't believe in infant baptism."

Mrs. Gorby pushed her cart forward. "Bye, I don't want to block the aisle."

I'm going to stop Grace from babysitting again. The very idea—baptizing our baby behind our *backs, thought Cheryl.*

Grandparents—a Special Role

"May you live to see your children's children" (Psalm 128:6a). This verse is the final one in a psalm enumerating blessing after blessing granted by God. Our grandchildren are a blessing.

Role Granted to Us

Our place in our grandchild's life is one the parents grant to us. Remember Naomi. Ruth 4:16 tells us, "Then Naomi took the child, laid him in her lap and cared for him." Naomi's privilege to participate in the life of her grandson came because she developed a love relationship with the child's mother, Ruth. Most of us treasure the relationship we had as children with our grandparents. If our children loved their grandparents, they will feel eager for their own children to enjoy the same closeness. But we must not fail to recognize that parents control our access to our grandchildren. We need to please the parents and not run roughshod over their wishes.

Influencers Not Molders

In normal circumstances, grandparents are not the primary molders of their grandchildren. They are a powerful source of good influence, but not the molders. In cases of death or divorce, however, they may expand their role. When kids love their grandparents, they are reluctant to disappoint them. This fact gives us influence with them. Also adding to our influence is the plus that they usually don't see us

123

as an authority role to rebel against while establishing their independence.

Help the Parents

Clear Away Hazards

Take a look around the house and change anything dangerous for the children. It's not necessary to redecorate when the grandchildren arrive, but we need to rethink where we keep our medicines and our poisons such as toilet bowl cleaner. Relocating the lead crystal and antique porcelain to higher shelves also helps everyone to relax.

Judy felt hurt when her son and his wife began staying in a motel instead of their home when they came for a visit. But the stacks of old magazines, boxes of buttons, and dishes of pennies all in ready reach of crawlers and toddlers made the visit feel more like a police action than a pleasure. Since the grandparents wouldn't clear away the hazards, the family resorted to motel visits.

Give Time, Have Fun

Babysitting is a great way to develop closeness. Volunteer. Invite the children on outings. Grandchildren don't need fancy entertainment. They need our time. Try coloring together or assembling puzzles. Sharing any activity forms bonds. Be sure to clear the plans and timing with the parents. Avoid disappointment for all by first discussing outings with the parents before promising the kids something that won't work after all.

Make Grandma's house intriguing by keeping some

toys on hand. Get out old toys left from your kid's childhood. Occasionally buy a few new ones that are age appropriate to generate fresh excitement about coming to Grandma's. Numerous, expensive toys aren't necessary. The fun comes from playing with ones that are different from the ones in their own home.

When the children visit, take the time to show them souvenirs from their parent's childhood. Teach them some of the games we played with our kids. Tell them stories about when we or mom and dad were children.

If we live a long way from the grandkids, send cards, read stories onto a tape, and write letters. I fondly remember a great aunt I only saw perhaps once every two years. She wrote small notes addressed just to me on tiny note paper in tiny envelopes. I thought she was wonderful because she made me feel special. If we live at a distance, make the most of our visits. Treasure participating in the routines: the evening bath, dressing time in the morning, and breakfast. We don't often share such daily duties with in-town grandchildren, yet ordinary routines contain the potential for special memories for both us and our grandkids.

Supply Encouragement

Unlike parents, grandparents don't have to notice everything amiss. Instead we major on accepting these precious personalities just as they are and encouraging them to like themselves.

Our primary role is not to teach but to enjoy, taking care, of course, not to sabotage whatever discipline the parents are establishing. Since we are not the front line disciplinarians, we are empowered to enhance the grandchildren's self-image.

Areas of Caution

Decisions

❖ *Rose and Dee* ❖

"You must not give that medicine to little Elizabeth. It has dreadful side effects that could damage her for the rest of her life." Dee was practically crying over the phone as she talked to her daughter-in-law.

"But Mother Dee, the disease she has carries terrible side effects that could damage her also."

"Don't do a thing until you read the literature about that dangerous medicine. I'll fax it to you. When you read it you'll see I'm right."

Being dutiful parents who certainly did not wish to expose their child to dangerous medicine, Rose and her husband waited to receive and read the literature. Next, they prayed about the matter. Then, they consulted with their doctor again. Satisfied the medicine was the best course to follow, they gave the first dose.

Hardly had Elizabeth swallowed the spoonful, when the phone rang. Unable to accept the parents' decision, Dee and her husband climbed into their car and drove the 200 miles to argue their case. In person, they wore their son down. Another doctor called into the case wrote a prescription for a second best medicine. Fortunately the child recovered completely, but Rose never recovered from her resentment of her mother-in-law's interference with their decision.

God gave these precious treasures to our child and spouse, not to us. They make the decisions. Our hope is for an atmosphere of open communication allowing us to express our opinions sometimes. Even our actions at the time of the baby's birth can determine how receptive the young parents are to our thoughts.

When the baby is born, where do the parents want us? One mother still rankles because her mother-in-law stayed too close to the delivery room, came to the hospital too often, and stayed too long after her difficult delivery. It's often guess work on our part to know what pleases, but asking may help eliminate the guessing. Even when bringing gifts to the newborn or at other times, it's wise to determine that the item isn't something they eagerly desired to buy for themselves or the other in-laws already planned to give.

Another major decision is schooling—private, public, or home-schooling. Some grandparents help pay for school expenses. The money must not represent an attempt to wring a certain decision from our young family. Rather, beneficial help enables the parents to pursue the choice they already wanted. The same caution applies to camps, sport activities, art or music lessons.

Uphold Parental Authority

✧ Eliza ✧

"I really wanted your dad to marry Rhea instead of your mother," Eliza remarked to her grandson, Shay. "I don't like the rules your *mother makes for you.*"

Shay looked down. His grandmother's words made him angry and uncomfortable. Since he knew he was supposed to respect Grandmother, he didn't know how to disagree with her. I guess I'll avoid her, he thought.

By criticizing Shay's mother, his grandmother risked damaging his mother's authority in his life.

"Children, obey your parents in the Lord, for this is right. 'Honor your father and mother'—which is the first commandment with a promise" (Ephesians 6:1-2). As grandparents, we honor and never undermine the parents' authority. Eventually, we reap the same sorrows as the parents if the children do not respect and obey them. Our best course backs up the parents' authority for our grandchild. We never allow ourselves to become a wedge against it.

Discipline

Irene told me, "My husband's mother can handle my daughter better than I can. I'm glad to have her around, because she's good for Suzy's behavior."

Ellie said, "I wish my mother-in-law would leave the psychology of my kids to me."

Which attitude represents your family? Find out and respect it.

"He who spares the rod hates his son, but he who loves him is careful to discipline him" (Proverbs 13:24). It pains grandparents to see their grandchild disciplined. Watching the child escape needed discipline causes as much pain. "Discipline your son, for in that there is hope; do not be a willing party to his death" (Proverbs 19:18). Mom and Dad often find it difficult enough to agree on when, what, and how much discipline is needed, let alone getting all the grandparents to also agree. Here, again, it's the parent's decision. We hope they listen to our concerns sometimes; but, standards for discipline belong to them.

Proverbs 1:33 says, "but whoever listens to me will live in safety and be at ease, without fear of harm." If we pray, we can relax and trust God to protect and quiet our fears for our grandchildren. Then, we can close our mouths before speaking rash words stemming from fear.

One area, however, where grandparents need the authority to discipline is if they are going to babysit a child, especially if on a regular basis. Immediate discipline is more effective than discipline administered hours later when Mom and Dad return. On the other hand as grandparents, we do not need to establish the same degree of authority as the parents in the child's life. We can try lots of distractions and alternatives before actually disciplining and at the same time uphold the parents' rules and not allow bad habits to take hold.

While we seek to uphold the parents' approach to raising their children, that does not mean that we must only hold to those rules when the grandchildren visit us. It's hopeless to embark on establishing certain table manners, for instance, if the parents don't care enough to reinforce the custom. At the same time, grandparents can hold out a higher standard by saying, "At our house, we do things this way." Fortunately, allowing grandchildren to make a shambles of our home isn't part of the package. When grandchildren visit our home, we can feel free to express basic ground rules. If we make our wishes known in a nice polite way with a smile on our faces, everyone will feel more willing to comply.

Favoritism

Of course, grandmothers should know to guard against showing partiality from one child to another. If Grandma succumbs to the temptation to indulge one grandchild more than the others, she sows seeds of envy, jealousy and resentment—not the crops thinking grandmas want to grow. If one child's personality is more ingratiating than another, we can determine to spend plenty of time with the more difficult child as he may need our love and approval the most. Also, we are alert to not show partiality to in-town grandchildren, making out-of-town grandchildren feel they are less important to us or vice versa.

Liz still curdles when she remembers her mother-in-law saying to one of her children, "Your sister knows how to act, so I'll take her to the museum." Liz spent the afternoon consoling the left out sibling, angry at the resentment she saw building between the children because of Grandma's comment.

Gifts

Presents work a wonderful bond between people. How much is too much? My correspondents disagreed. Some complained about lavish gifts. Some were grateful. Asking is the safest path. If we live in town, few parents would relish us showing up with gifts every time we come. Kids who expect gifts are developing unfortunate attitudes. Be thoughtful. It's hard for our daughter-in-law to muster up enthusiasm over gifts with 120 pieces. Everyone knows who will do the most pick-up duty. Secure permission before giving loud, noisy toys that can grate on the nerves.

If we come from afar, however, gifts help cement relationships. If some grandchildren live close by and some are far away, we need to be careful that gifts appear to be equal.

Claudia couldn't afford to buy lavish gifts for her grandchildren, but she enjoyed shopping garage sales and finding bargain treasures to give them. The children didn't care if they were second hand because they were new to them and in relatively good condition.

One mother said, "I really appreciate the gifts my mother-in-law brings. We depend on her generosity to clothe the children. I just wish, sometimes, she would allow me to go with her to pick them out. Since we can't afford to buy much, I'd really enjoy the fun of choosing."

What about candy and chewing gum? Some parents delight in them; some abhor them; all kids love them. Respect the parents' wishes and use moderation. "It is not good to eat too much honey" (Proverbs 25:27a). Certainly it is not good too close to mealtime.

Criticism

Leah frowned when Sonny stomped his foot then ran from the house, slamming the door after him. "You're raising a brat," Leah told her daughter-in-law.

Since children are an extension of a parent, people don't take kindly to criticism of their offspring. Criticism from a grandparent stirs up additional problems. Our children may have doubts about their ability to live up to our expectations of them as parents. Because of the conflicting philosophies and pressures in today's society, parents most likely experience doubts about their abilities to raise their children. Since criticism from us may confirm their worst fears, we don't want them avoiding us because we make them feel inadequate for the job. Remember the molding of children is a process; it is not finished at age two, or five, or eight. At all ages the developing child still requires refining and maturing.

Granny Webber called her grandchildren regularly to complain about their behavior. When they were older, she couldn't understand why they rarely wanted to visit her and had little to say when they did. Her complaints changed from their behavior to their lack of visits.

By remembering life's pace during children's active teen years, we will understand the scarcity of time available for us and refrain from criticizing the infrequency of their visits. We convey love and interest, but avoid demands.

Remember the grandchildren will probably quote us to their parents so keep everything quotable. One grandmother was chagrined to learn her grandchild had reported her remark, "I hope they paint their house white this time."

We mothers-in-law walk a fine line, don't we? Required equipment for our role: weather vanes to determine the prevailing winds of our family, antenna to detect the static from our words or actions, a reverse gear to quickly apologize and back track. Where do we get a mental weather vane and the other equipment? Through prayer.

Spiritual Influence

Prayer

I wonder how many people are in heaven as the result of praying grandparents. We won't know on this earth what dangers our grandchildren avoid or what blessings they attain because of our prayers. "The children of your servants will live in your presence; their descendants will be established before you" (Psalm 102:28).

This promise for our grandchildren to be established before God is worth prayer. While we don't want to overrule the parents, as Grace did at the beginning of the chapter, we can talk to the children about Jesus. We can take them to church with the approval of their parents. We can make the books and videos we give Christian ones. We can make sure the ones at our house are Christian.

Pray for wisdom for the parents to raise and guide their children. Pray by name every day for each grandchild. Pray for each child to follow the Lord and give God first place in his heart. Pray that they will delight to walk in His path and do His will, that they will discern the ways of the world and turn from them, that they will not be snared in the mindset of the world. Pray for their protection from disease, accidents, and ungodly thinking.

Grandparents are important to the emotional development of the grandchildren. Do everything possible to please the parents with your relationship to their children. Enjoy them fully. Kindness toward grandchildren softens the hearts of parents and wins love.

- ✧ Enjoy grandchildren as encouragers, not molders.
- ✧ Make our house safe and fun for grandchildren.
- ✧ Respect the parents' wishes.
- ✧ Watch out for two 'isms'—favoritism and criticism.
- ✧ Pray for grandchildren.

✧ *Eleven* ✧

Dealing with Discouraging Situations

✧ **Dorothy** ✧

"Art, what a nice surprise. It's been so long since you called." Dorothy smiled into the phone and motioned for her husband, Merle, to pick up the extension to talk to their son.

Art launched into an account of his latest triumphant presentation before the board of supervisors.

"Wait a minute, Art. What's the loud noise in the background? I can't understand what you're saying over the racket." Dorothy strained to hear his answer.

"Arlene," she heard Art say, and something else, but she couldn't distinguish the words. Finally, she said, "We'll hang up and let you call right back,

Art. This is a bad phone connection."

She hung up. Merle came in and sat beside her on the sofa. "Don't wait on Art to call back, honey. I caught what he said. Arlene got on their extension and turned up the TV full blast to prevent Art from talking to us."

Dorothy looked at him with her mouth open. "But we are his parents."

"I guess we've realized for a long time, Art's wife doesn't want him talking to his parents."

"But it's been a year and a half since we've talked to our son."

❖ Marilyn ❖

"Joel, Dad has a business trip next week to a plant within a few miles of your house. I'd like to come with him and stop in the evening to see you and your little ones. Would it be okay?" Marilyn wished she could keep the pleading sound out of her voice.

"Uh, I, well, I guess you'd better not. Paula would get upset."

"But Joel, we haven't seen your children for two years. We understand Paula not wanting to make the drive here. But we'll be right in your town," Marilyn protested over the rising lump in her throat. "Maybe we could meet you and the children somewhere instead. Paula wouldn't have to come."

"It isn't worth the guff I'd take. Uh, I need to hang up now."

"Wait, Joel. We want to see you."

As the phone went dead, Marilyn wished her ache would die as easily.

Difficult to Bear

Some mothers-in-law find themselves in grievous situations carrying grave consequences. Some mothers are stuck with totally undeserved difficulties trying to relate to unreasonable in-laws. What are women to do if they find themselves in sad situations not of their own making? Many times the unfortunate mother can't win. No matter what she does, it's wrong. Isaiah 43:19 offers hope: "See, I am doing a new thing! Now it springs up; do you not perceive it? I am making a way in the desert and streams in the wasteland."

God knows the way through our personal desert. When either our child or child's spouse suffers from psychological disorders, extreme immaturity, or self-ishness, family relationships become difficult in spite of Mom's best efforts. Even if our in-law's hostility prevents us from having contact with our child or grandchildren, even if someone is involved in sub-stance abuse, or marital infidelity, the Lord can help us rise above the situation and prevent the waters of discouragement from overflowing us. "When you pass through the waters, I will be with you; and when you pass through the rivers, they will not sweep over you. When you walk through the fire, you will not be burned; the flames will not set you ablaze" (Isaiah 43:2).

Impossible to Please

It helps to remember many of these sad situations are inherited from the in-law's dysfunctional family. It is not a personal thing against us, but rather a further extension of poor relationship skills already in effect. Sometimes the mother-in-law is the scapegoat when in reality the trouble lies between the husband and wife.

Some children who experienced strong dependency, overdo their independence when they finally break free, hurting their parents by mistaking the throwing off of family ties for emotional freedom. God can use us to "bind up the brokenhearted, to proclaim freedom for the captives and release from darkness for the prisoners," (Isaiah 61:1b). Perhaps our difficult place is a trust from God to open the way for His healing.

On the other hand, what do we do if we suddenly realize we have caused problems and contributed to the strained relationship which is causing us grief? What if we recognize ourselves in a portion of some of the stories in this book, and suspect, however unintentionally, we've added to the problems? What then? Isaiah 41:10 says, "So do not fear, for I am with you; do not be dismayed, for I am your God. I will strengthen you and help you; I will uphold you with my righteous right hand."

Steps to Try

Apologize

Don't worry about who is right and wrong. A good apology carries power and is worth trying. "I tell you the truth, unless a grain of wheat falls to the ground and dies, it remains only a single seed. But if it dies, it produces many seeds" (John 12:24). Apology, which causes something in us to die, bears fruit. Our children have flaws. Some flaws probably cause marriage stress. Which of us has done the perfect job of raising our children? Moms can apologize for whatever failings survived our mothering efforts. As the saying goes—take the hit, or accept the blame. Allow our shoulders to take the responsibility.

Forgive

In Matthew 18:21 Peter asks Jesus if he should forgive seven times. In verse 22, Jesus answers, "not seven times, but seventy-seven times." Some of you may feel you're getting close to that number. To resist forgiving won't solve the problems and causes us real harm. Unforgiveness is like acid spilled on a budding garden. Forgiveness enables us to sow mercy which brings a good harvest—eventually. "Get rid of all bitterness, rage and anger, brawling and slander, along with every form of malice. Be kind and compassionate to one another, forgiving each other, just as in Christ God forgave you" (Ephesians 4:31-32).

Stretching to forgive creates elasticity in our personality. Pizza dough stretched into a circle makes a delicious base for the filling. When we are stretched in forgiveness, we become more and more able to hold God's wonderful fillings. "Let not mercy and truth forsake thee: bind them about thy neck; write them upon the table of thine heart" (Proverbs 3:3, KJV). Mercy keeps our hearts soft and helps us forgive even when we don't like the truth we see. "Bear with each other and forgive whatever grievances you may have against one another. Forgive as the Lord forgave you"

139

(Colossians 3:13). "But God demonstrates his own love for us in this: While we were still sinners, Christ died for us" (Romans 5:8). Jesus didn't allow our sin to prevent Him from dying for us. If He died for our in-law's unfortunate qualities, we can manage, with His help, to forgive.

Watch Our Words

"He who guards his mouth and his tongue keeps himself from calamity" (Proverbs 21:23). We grow in self-discipline when we cannot freely express ourselves. "Through patience a ruler can be persuaded, and a gentle tongue can break a bone" (Proverbs 25:15). Pray for a gentle tongue to break through the bone of tough situations.

"Do not rebuke a mocker or he will hate you" (Proverbs 9:8a). Don't waste words when they won't be heard. Winnie told me, "All my conversations with my children and their spouses are polite nothings, not real or honest. They are so lacking in depth, I could talk to total strangers and say the same things."

Another mother explained, "Our talk is only surface stuff, because when I open my mouth, they close their ears. It's lonely. An idea is doomed if I suggest it."

If we are burning to tell our in-laws a thing or two, go tell it to a tree. It does as much good, and a lot less harm. Better yet, tell it to the Lord. He understands. He has the power to change the situation and to enable us to endure meanwhile.

Offer Love

Remember Dorothy in the first story of this chapter?

Later, she lovingly told her daughter-in-law that her son was all hers. "I give him to you," she said. Then she continued to show gracious interest in Arlene. Gradually the girl felt less threatened and the situation mended. Ask for wisdom for how to convey love. Even if it's rebuffed, love penetrates.

Monica dealt in a similar fashion with her daughter-in-law, Candy. Whenever Monica began talking with her son, Paul, Candy would get between them and begin kissing Paul until the conversation stopped. Month after month, Candy effectively prevented Monica from having any conversation with Paul. Finally, Monica realized the girl was competing with her, Paul's mother, for Paul's attention rather than demonstrating unusual ardor. With a mighty bite on her tongue, Monica restricted her conversation to topics that involved and interested Monica. After a while Monica felt included and stopped her adolescent smooching.

"But love your enemies, do good to them, and lend to them without expecting to get anything back. Then your reward will be great, and you will be sons of the Most High, because he is kind to the ungrateful and wicked. Be merciful, just as your Father is merciful" (Luke 6:35-36).

Promote Family Gatherings

✧ Sadie ✧

"My first daughter-in-law resents the second daughter-in-law. I ignore the situation and pretend everything is fine. For Thanksgiving the whole family accepted my dinner invitation. We all ig-

nored the fact that Chelsea wouldn't speak to her sister-in-law. At least the rest of us were able to enjoy each other. Maybe, after enough time, Chelsea will put aside her jealousy of her new sister-in-law."

"Do not withhold good from those who deserve it, when it is in your power to act" (Proverbs 3:27). Every opportunity to sow acceptance and love by bringing the family together tears down walls of misunderstanding, walls of distrust. Family gatherings offer opportunities to build acceptance.

Maybe we feel as if our family doesn't deserve our great efforts to organize and prepare a get-together. Who of us deserved the love of our Saviour? "Bless those who persecute you; bless and do not curse" (Romans 12:14).

Perhaps our invitations have been ignored or rebuffed. When we experience serious family schisms, holidays and birthdays make us vulnerable to self-pity or depression. By recognizing that possibility, we can plan ahead to brighten the day with other pleasant activity.

Adopt Healthy Attitudes

How we choose to look at a difficulty influences how we endure it and rise above it. By remaining positive we protect our own mental health. We sin when we complain, criticize, and worry. We need to exert caution to avoid coming across as having all the answers. Remember Proverbs 3:7-8: "Do not be wise in your own eyes; fear the LORD and shun evil. This will bring health to your body and nourishment to your bones."

Don't Project Fears into the Future

"Therefore do not worry about tomorrow, for tomorrow will worry about itself. Each day has enough trouble of its own" (Matthew 6:34). Borrowing trouble and projecting our fears into the future makes any load heavier to carry. The temptation in a difficult situation is to think it will continue into the future forever, becoming worse and worse. By committing our heartaches to God and believing He will improve the situation in His timing, we make room for peace and joy to grow today. Since we can't control the future, anyway, worrying over it won't help. Regardless of the horrible fears we have, or the dreads we harbor, we don't profit from dwelling on them. God controls every facet of our lives, and we grow tall and strong in faith from believing Him to help us.

Ask God's Help

Distance ourselves from the situation by giving ourselves breaks from confronting the problem or thinking about it. Resist the urge to pry. Sometimes it's healthier for a mother-in-law not to know too much. "Do not pay attention to every word people say, or you may hear your servant cursing you" (Ecclesiastes 7:21). If our child is satisfied with the situation, we can try to accept and ignore it.

Ask God's help to provide an example of Christ to our in-laws. We may be the only person to demonstrate the gospel to them. Like Psalm 57:7, we can say, "My heart is steadfast, O God, my heart is steadfast; I will sing and make music." Only Christ can give us the strength and desire to sing in the middle of problems. By doing so, we can be a mirror to reflect Christ's love to those around us.

"If God is for us, who can be against us?" (Romans 8:31b). When we align ourselves with God, the forces of evil cannot destroy us.

Focus on Hope

"And we rejoice in the hope of the glory of God. Not only so, but we also rejoice in our sufferings, because we know that suffering produces perseverance; perseverance, character; and character, hope. And hope does not disappoint us, because God has poured out his love into our hearts by the Holy Spirit, whom he has given us" (Romans 5:2b-5).

We grow in trials. They cause us to draw closer to God; and hence, we learn more about His character. The more we know Him the more we fall in love with Him. Hard places develop character. Loving the unlovable is a greater challenge than loving those who love us. "But I say unto you, Love your enemies, bless them that curse you, do good to them that hate you, and pray for them which despitefully use you, and persecute you" (Matthew 5:44, KJV). Are we allowing God's love for us to pour out of us and into those family members who have caused us so much pain?

"Yet the LORD longs to be gracious to you; he rises to show you compassion. For the LORD is a God of justice. Blessed are all who wait for him! . . . You will weep no more. How gracious he will be when you cry for help! As soon as he hears, he will answer you"

(Isaiah 30:18-19). He loves us and hears us. Even though the answer may not always be to our liking, He dries our tears.

It's God's battle. Our situation may seem hopeless just as it did for the Israelites when the water was before them and Pharaoh's army was behind them. "Moses answered the people, 'Do not be afraid. Stand firm and you will see the deliverance the LORD will bring you today. The Egyptians you see today you will never see again. The LORD will fight for you; you need only to be still" (Exodus 14:13-14). How hard it is to be still. Our outward actions may be quiet, but only our hope in God allows us to be calm on the inside.

"Though the fig-tree does not bud and there are no grapes on the vines, though the olive crop fails and the fields produce no food, though there are no sheep in the pen and no cattle in the stalls, yet I will rejoice in the LORD, I will be joyful in God my Saviour. The Sovereign LORD is my strength; he makes my feet like the feet of a deer, he enables me to go on the heights" (Habakkuk 3:17-19b). Our circumstances may not change, but God will see us through hurtful times.

Stay Busy

"No temptation has seized you except what is common to man. And God is faithful; he will not let you be tempted beyond what you can bear. But when you are tempted, he will also provide a way out so that you can stand up under it" (1 Corinthians 10:13). Find outlets for our energies. Develop a repertoire of distracting, pleasant things to do to change the directions of our thoughts, to prevent dwelling on our troubles. Look around and find a worse situation. There are always some. Help those people if we can. Be grateful we aren't in those situations. Practice regular thanksgiving for even the smallest blessings. Find a friend who won't gossip to share your sorrow or fears when they weigh too heavy.

✧ Claudia ✧

Claudia looked away as her friend, Janet, read a paragraph from her son's letter to the five ladies gathered in the lounge of the retirement home where they lived. Blinking rapidly, she tried to prevent tears from forming.

It didn't work. "What's the matter, Claudia?" Nita asked.

"I don't want to think about it, but it hurts so much." The pent up dam burst, and Claudia poured out her story.

"Thirty years ago, my daughter-in-law grew cold to me. I never knew why. One day my son told me they were thinking about moving." Claudia's voice trembled. "Suddenly they were gone. They never told me where."

Janet slipped her letter back into her pocket.

"I tried to call and I wrote to their old home," Claudia moaned. "I never found them. They just vanished. It's 30 years. I don't even know if they are living.

The ladies leaned close to hear Claudia.

"I loved my three grandchildren. They were small

then. I guess the children think I didn't care, that
I abandoned them."

Nita fished a packet of Kleenex from her purse.
"We never guessed. Now I understand why you're
so compassionate," she said.

"I feel better just from telling you," responded
Claudia.

We need the support of others when we hurt.

Times to Intervene

There are times when holding our peace is not
appropriate, and we must enter the fray. Only we, with
God's help, can determine when to intervene. In order
to filter out any improper motivation, sincere prayer
precedes our stepping into the situation. Wisdom
suggests first seeking the counsel of our pastor and
others familiar with God's ways. Consider intervening
when there is suspicion of child abuse—physical but
also emotional. Where there is neglect or malnutri-
tion, we need to step in. Wife abuse requires steps
also. It's a fine line to determine what constitutes
abuse, hence the need for prayer and counsel.

There are degrees of interfering. Begin with the
least, progressing to stronger measures only if required. We can comfort ourselves with the thought in
Psalm 72:14: "He will rescue them from oppression
and violence, for precious is their blood in his sight."

Also consider, "In this you greatly rejoice, though
now for a little while you may have had to suffer grief
in all kinds of trials. These have come so that your
faith—of greater worth than gold, which perishes even

though refined by fire—may be proved genuine and may result in praise, glory and honor when Jesus Christ is revealed" (1 Peter 1:6-7). God may be refining us and our family.

When situations with our in-laws discourage and dishearten us, we remember that God understands our grief, because He came in the form of man and experienced life in the flesh. He cares about our distress and will use it for our growth in Christ-like qualities. Our trials, then, equip us to help others.

- ❖ Apologize readily.
- ❖ Forgive quickly.
- ❖ Speak cautiously.
- ❖ Love lavishly.
- ❖ Pray for healthy attitudes.
- ❖ Pray for hope.
- ❖ Keep busy.
- ❖ Intervene only when led by God.

✧ *Twelve* ✧

Caring Even through Divorce

✧ **Mary Alice** ✧

"Another fight?" Mary Alice looked at her son Reed's stormy face. "You and Ellen fight all the time."

"Not all the time, Mom, just when the money gets tight," Reed said as he shrugged his shoulders.

"I know a good lawyer; why don't you talk to him? He dissolves marriages painlessly." Mary Alice pulled the phone book out of the drawer.

"Mom, you've offered to give me a lawyer's name a hundred times. You'd think you want me to leave Ellen."

"I'm tired of seeing you angry all the time. Here's the number."

"Well, I'm mad today." Reed took the phone book

and began to dial the number. "We do fight a lot,"
he said as he put the receiver to his ear.

We want our conduct and conversation to lessen the pressures on the marriage, not increase them. We certainly don't want to contribute to a divorce.

If our failure to let go plays a part in the dissolution of our child's marriage, we will live with regrets—ours and our child's. Our goal is to see the child's marriage succeed even if we regret our child's choice of spouse, and even if we see our child is miserable in his marriage. God forbid we deal the marriage a fatal blow. Mark 10:9 says, "Therefore what God has joined together, let man [or mother, we might add,] not separate." We do not want to deliver the blow that separates the couple.

In *Parade Magazine,* Milton Berle is quoted by Dotson Rader citing his mother as a factor in his divorce. "But I don't think she [his wife] could go up against my mother, who was much stronger. I was the man who walked the tightrope. All because my mother never wanted me to get married, and I was in love with Joyce."

Another mother prayed every day that God would take her son away from "that woman" he married. The bride did not know about the prayers for many years, but she sensed the attitude. The two women never became friends.

We're Getting a Divorce, Mom

These words have unleased floods of disbelief, grief, fear, and anger in the hearts of countless mothers.

Women suffer tumultuous emotions during the first months after their child and spouse separate. Many told me their only comfort was the Bible and clinging to the knowledge God was good even if the world around them tilted in a crazy spin. "The LORD is close to the brokenhearted and saves those who are crushed in spirit" (Psalm 34:18). The first year was the hardest all agreed. As difficult as the news was to bear at first, God comforted them as time progressed; and they grew skilled in drawing comfort from God. "And call upon me in the day of trouble; I will deliver you, and you will honor me" (Psalm 50:15). The women took solace in the fact that unlike Mary Alice in our story earlier, the divorce was not their decision nor even their failure. During the first difficult days, women reported it was important to guard their words for the sake of future relationships. In the first shock of the news, a mom's hasty talk can inflict additional harm to the already wounded couple.

"Grab hold of God as fast as you can, and pray fervently," Marjorie told me. "The news is as devastating as a death in the family. We need God's help to survive it and to prevent irreparable mistakes with how we react."

Mothers have reported two types of reactions. If the offended one was their own child, then anger, resentment and defensiveness loomed. If the offending one was their own child, many disclosed they were suspicious that others criticized them as mothers. These women battled feelings of somehow failing as mothers since divorce occurred. "'No weapon forged against you will prevail, and you will refute every tongue that accuses you. This is the heritage of the servants of the LORD, and this is their vindication from me,' declares the LORD" (Isaiah 54:17). We should not go out and verbally debate with our accusers, yet we can refute them through our actions and attitudes. Our meek and quiet spirit, as we go about the daily duties of life, can show others that we are a true servant of the Lord. "For he stands at the right hand of the needy one, to save his life from those who condemn him" (Psalm 109:31). By holding tightly to God's words, we can hold ourselves apart from condemnation, even the kind we put on ourselves.

If Grandchildren Are Involved

Grandchildren Need to Feel Loved

The security of the children is shored up if grandparents from both sides of the family continue their contact as before the separation. Grandparents can encourage aunts, uncles and cousins to also invest time in the children. Take every opportunity to show and tell the children that no matter what their parents may do or say, we will always love them. We can send little love notes or cards to them on any plain, ordinary day. We can call them to tell them we love them and ask about their interests. Depending on their ages and personalities, we can take each individual child on an outing all their own.

A mother-in-law helps when upholding the authority of both parents. Speaking ill of the in-law only creates insecurity for the children. A child's sense of identity as a worthy person is closely tied to his image of his parents. If we run down one parent, we risk the child deciding, "Since there's something wrong with my parent, there must be something wrong with me." Not to mention criticism jeopardizes the custody-holding parent's willingness to allow grandparent visits.

Grandchildren Need Both Parents

✧ *Helen* ✧

"I can't believe you'd bring your father back here after what he did to this family!" Helen sputtered when her granddaughter, Doris, explained the plans she had for her father.

"Why, the man abandoned you and your sisters 30 years ago, and you haven't heard a word from him since."

"But he's our dad, Grandma," Doris tried to explain.

"Your grandfather and I were the ones who raised you. What would have happened to you if we hadn't stepped in when your father vanished off the face of the earth? I still can't believe the four of you kids flew to see him—all the way to Montana, for heavens sake. Spent pockets full of money to see a derelict on his death bed. Now you want to bring him here?" Helen shook her head.

"Grandma, because of what Dad did, we hardly knew our father. We needed to at least see him before he died. He is part of who we are. We needed to know him. Anyway, he was so surprised to see us and find out we cared about him after all these years, he's getting well, instead of dying like the hospital thought," Doris beamed. Reluctantly Helen smiled.

Even if we consider one of our grandchildren's parents a scoundrel, the children need a relationship with both parents unless they pose a danger like physical abuse. In situations where either physical or mental child abuse exists, the contact does more harm than good. We need to understand the child's need for an on-going relationship. If the absent parent neglects contacting the child, grandparents can fill some of the gap with love and attention.

But What Helps Me?

Forgiveness

"Make every effort to live in peace with all men and to be holy; without holiness no one will see the Lord. See to it that no one misses the grace of God and that no bitter root grows up to cause trouble and defile many" (Hebrews 12:14-15). God helps us forgive when we ask Him. Our attitudes are healed when we forgive, helping us walk through the debris left in the wake of a divorce without bitterness taking root.

We probably have an incomplete picture of the events, actions, and reactions causing the divorce. "Therefore judge nothing before the appointed time; wait till the Lord comes. He will bring to light what is hidden in darkness and will expose the motives of men's hearts. At that time each will receive his praise from God" (1 Corinthians 4:5). Leave the judging of the mess to God. Free from placing blame, we can love.

Forgiveness clears the lines of communication. "Their sins and lawless acts I will remember no more" (Hebrews 10:17). Because God forgives our sin, we should let go of our in-law's offenses. The first step in this direction is to stop talking and thinking about the offense. Crowd it out with constructive thoughts.

Communication

If there are grandchildren involved in the divorce, for their sakes, we try to communicate regularly and kindly with whoever has custody. One woman said, "Put your feelings aside for the sake of the kids."

Another woman said, "For the luxury of saying what I'd like to say, I'd risk destroying my opportunity to benefit my grandchildren. It's not worth it."

Many mothers-in-law won gratitude by continuing to send cards to the divorced in-law. Many telephoned periodically to keep the estranged spouse abreast of family news, births, etc. A couple of girls expressed gratitude for being invited to family reunions. One mother-in-law said, "Of course we want you to come to the reunion. As the mother of our grandchildren you're part of the family."

Another told her son-in-law, "I love you and consider you family. If you are divorcing me, you'll have to tell me. Let me know if you want it different."

When maintaining a relationship with a divorced in-law, make sure your own child understands your actions. Celia said her mother explained she was not taking sides or putting the in-law's interests ahead of Celia's. She simply was pursuing what was a happy friendship, and she didn't want it to stop. After explaining that she thought it also in the best interest of the grandchildren, she asked Celia if she objected.

Another mother-in-law reported she stayed in pleasant contact with the parents of her daughter-in-law and is sometimes invited to spend Christmas day with the family.

A number of young people reported they were glad "Not to be dropped like a hot potato." We can help bring serenity as Matthew 5:9 says: "Blessed are the peacemakers, for they will be called sons of God."

Love

✧ *Jolene and Shelley* ✧

"The children are crying," Shelley's voice was low over the phone. Jolene, her mother-in-law, strained to hear. "They're hungry, yet I can't force myself out of bed long enough to fix dinner. I tried at lunch, but after getting out the bread and peanut butter, I went back to bed. Little Jenny tried to make sandwiches for the other children."

The desperate tone in Shelley's voice alarmed Jolene. She knew her daughter-in-law was devastated when Allen left her. Jolene also felt devastated after her son, Allen, left his family. She didn't understand why Allen forced Shelley and the five children to leave his house. Now they practically lived in squalor. With a sigh, Jolene picked up her purse and headed for the wretched family.

After fixing, serving and cleaning up dinner, she sat at her daughter-in-law's bedside. "I'm going to help you, dear. Together, we'll take care of this family until you can gather your strength from this terrible blow, find a job, and get on your feet."

✧ *Harriet and Emma* ✧

"I'm not letting the kids visit your house any more," Harriet told her mother-in-law, Emma. *"You sent them home with vomit still on the clothes in their suitcase. Why didn't you tell me they were sick this weekend?"* Harriet continued to vent her anger. *"The last time they visited, you cut the girls' hair. They were so upset with their uneven, short hair they cried and put paper bags over their heads. How could you cut their hair without asking me or listening to them say they didn't want haircuts?"*

"We have court-ordered visitation rights," Emma cut into her daughter-in-law's tirade.

"Remember what you told the judge in court?" Harriet lashed out. *"You told him from now on Harriet doesn't exist. If I don't exist, you'll have to talk to someone else about seeing the children."*

Love changes people more than words. Loving someone who has wounded our family presents a challenge. God is equal to the challenge. My questionnaires brought amazing examples of women who persevered in love in spite of their natural feelings. They allowed the love of Christ to go through them, and they demonstrated the love of God to their in-laws. He empowers people to love when it seems impossible.

Prayer

✧ *Sandra* ✧

"Look, Bryce is standing by the tool display."

Sandra pointed out their ex-son-in-law to her husband as they entered the hardware store. "Let's come back later. I never want to see him again. It was good riddance when he dropped out of our daughter's life."

"He's a cad all right," Dave agreed.

Just then Bryce turned and saw them. Surprising herself, Sandra ran to him and threw her arms around him mumbling something about good to see him.

"Let's start praying daily for Bryce's salvation," Sandra said when she and Dave left the store.

A year later, Sandra and Dave responded to a knock at their front door. There stood Bryce. "I've come to beg your forgiveness for the way I treated your daughter. I've become a Christian since I last saw you. I'm sorry I hurt everybody. I wanted to apologize to you."

"Bless those who curse you, pray for those who mistreat you" (Luke 6:28). When a divorce tears a family, prayer is the route to peace. We need God's viewpoint toward the offending party. God hates people's sin, but He loves sinners, even when the sin is wounding our child and our grandchildren.

When our child was the one who did the wounding, remember Samson. No doubt Samson's parents were disappointed with him. He destroyed a promising future by making poor choices. Yet in the end, Samson brought abundant damage to the enemies of God. The end is not yet written for our child. "But I will establish my covenant with you, and you will enter the ark—you and your sons and your wife and your sons' wives with you" (Genesis 6:18).

We can claim God's covenant to bring our sons and daughters and their spouses into the ark of salvation. We believe God keeps the promises of the Bible, so leave it to God whether or not the promise will be for our child and spouse as individuals or as a married couple. Prayer helps us shift the burden from our shoulders to God's capable shoulder. One son told his mother, "Mom, you're carrying my burden again, and I don't want you to do it." Prayer helps us from interfering where we aren't wanted.

What about Remarriage?

Regardless of the positions different churches take on the issue of divorce and remarriage, as mothers we want to maintain communication. The decision rests in the hands of our child, not in our hands. Caution is the best rule if our child or his or her ex-spouse begins to date again. Whoever the dates are, as human beings they're loved by God, and therefore, deserving of our respect. If it appears our child is repeating history with another unfortunate choice of companionship, discuss it with God. Running the person down only arouses defensiveness, making the attachment stronger.

If our child remarries, take care not to slight any children the new in-law brings from a previous marriage. Several daughters-in-law resented the new mother-in-law who either talked harshly to her children or ignored them. Others spoke with gratitude of the acceptance and affection shown her children from a previous marriage. Because of the mother-in-law's kindness, these women loved them.

The responses I gathered from Christian mothers whose children divorced were a testimony of the power of God to override our natural tendencies and supply supernatural grace when we need it. "Jesus looked at them and said, 'With man this is impossible, but not with God; all things are possible with God'" (Mark 10:27). With Him we can endure the heartbreak of divorce, demonstrate caring, and hope for a better end.

◇ Exert caution in our first reaction to our child's divorce plans.

◇ Give grandchildren extra support.

◇ Recognize the grandchildren's need for both parents.

◇ Forgive.

◇ Keep communication open.

◇ Ask God to help you love.

◇ Pray for God's best solutions.

✧ *Thirteen* ✧

Preparing for the Inevitable— Old Age

✧ Lucinda ✧

"I looked after you when you were small and helpless, so you owe it to me to take me in—"

"Now that I'm old," Mitchell finished his mother's sentence. *"Here we go again."*

"It's Thanksgiving, let's think about our blessings," April, Mitchell's wife, broke in hoping to rescue the dinner from the tiresome, old argument. *"I'm grateful we are all in such good health,"* April said, her smile a bit artificial.

"Speak for yourself," Lucinda said. *"My joints ache more every day. If you loved me, you would let me come live with you."*

"Mother, we've been over this a thousand times. You would not be happy here. Why even our

telephone ringing annoys you," Mitchell said.

"We plan to look after you, Mother Lucinda, when you need it," April said. "We won't neglect you. It's just that we think you'll enjoy life more if you aren't under our roof."

"You don't love me. You'll stick me in some awful nursing home."

"No awful places for you, Mother, including our own house. Now can we talk about something else?" Mitchell reached for the serving spoon.

✧ Ruth Ellen ✧

"Do you think you'd want the Wedgewood candy dish when I die?" Ruth Ellen asked her daughter-in-law, Nan. "Or should I give it to friends?"

"Whatever pleases you," Nan answered, searching her mind for a way to change the conversation.

"I don't think I'll leave you my silver tea set; you wouldn't bother to polish it. How about the still life over the sofa? It's my most valuable art, but I'm not sure you appreciate my things." Ruth Ellen frowned at Nan. "You never seem interested."

"Your things are lovely," Nan tried to sound enthusiastic. "It's just that when I visit I'd rather talk about you and what's happening in your life than your possessions. Why don't you make a list of who you want to inherit what?"

Plan Ahead for Old Age

"You have been faithful with a few things; I will put

you in charge of many things. Come and share your master's happiness!" (Matthew 25:21). If we think about the decisions old age requires before we are old, we are better prepared to make good decisions and less likely to make ones we regret. Emotionally based decisions aren't always rational and wise.

"Gray hair is a crown of splendor; it is attained by a righteous life" (Proverbs 16:31). We want righteousness established in our lives when we are old and gray.

Observe old people who gather a flock of admirers around them. What are the qualities making people want to spend time with them? Look at the ones who are lonely, what do they have in common? Let's begin now, at whatever our age, to enlarge our personalities in the characteristics which attract. "But strong meat belongeth to them that are of full age, even those who by reason of use have their senses exercised to discern both good and evil" (Hebrews 5:14 KJV). In order to arrive at old age with strong discernment of what attracts people, let's start while we are young exercising our senses to develop the characteristics which people appreciate.

Qualities That Bless in Old Age
Thankfulness

"Give thanks to the LORD, call on his name; make known among the nations what he has done" (Psalm 105:1). We pick people who exhibit thankfulness over complainers any time we have a choice of whom to visit. Verbalize thanks for favors and companionship. Smiles, hugs, notes and, most important, our words do the trick. When thankfulness for what's good in our lives dominates our thinking, a cheerfulness results. Cheerfulness attracts people. My mother provides our entire family with a wonderful inheritance by expressing gratitude to God in nearly every conversation.

Flexibility

Times change, medical practices change, styles change, and plans change. Accepting change, unless it's sinful, helps us relate to younger people. Adapt where possible. Stay informed with recent information instead of the knowledge we relied on years ago. Our children's lives will pass through the same phases ours did but with some new ones added due to changing times. If we adapt to change, we will experience more contentment.

Good Listening Skills

"Ears that hear and eyes that see—the LORD has made them both" (Proverbs 20:12). People enjoy the opportunity to express their thoughts, dreams, and ideas. If we develop skill in drawing out the thinking of people we talk with, they'll go away pleased. Notice how many people take the trouble to get you talking. Not many I'll wager. Some older people tend to focus conversations upon themselves, or talk at length about someone the listener doesn't even know. By too frequently injecting, "I remember" or, "Something like that happened to me" in our conversations, we will begin to dominate the conversation without realizing it. Frequent reminiscing causes the listener's eyes to glaze over. Give our listener permission to stop us if we repeat a story. No one enjoys the sixth repetition. The listener could tell the tale himself after hearing it the umpteenth time. Growing old doesn't entitle us to speak our mind regardless of the consequences—not if we want to continue the companionship. Hone our listening skills.

Unselfishness

"Do nothing out of selfish ambition or vain conceit, but in humility consider others better than yourselves" (Philippians 2:3). Self centered, in babyhood we squall when our will is crossed. The need to fight preoccupation with self follows us all our lives. Unquestionably self-importance doesn't attract a following.

Violet signed her correspondence as "Senior member" a reminder to the family that she was entitled to extra deference. Sometimes she signed, "the Family Octogenarian." Everyone knew she expected the most honored position and extra consideration at any gathering. No one minded, but voluntary respect beats demanded respect.

When we are old, our respect for others' busy schedules will prevent a demanding attitude. Advance planning protects us from requiring frequent, small errands on our behalf. If we make lists of what we need well in advance, the errand runner can combine them with his or her chores when convenient instead of making special trips.

When failing health narrows our world in old age, the temptation increases to focus on ourselves. By preferring others over ourselves, we slay selfishness before it can get a foothold and multiply. Cultivating genuine interest in others protects us.

Trust the Lord

"Even to your old age and gray hairs I am he, I am he who will sustain you. I have made you and I will carry you; I will sustain you and I will rescue you" (Isaiah 46:4). If we are anxious instead of trusting God, our children will try to protect us from worry. Their usual method is to not tell us about worrisome things, thus shutting us out of chunks of their lives. Better to begin now learning how to intercede for problems and leave the concerns with God instead of carrying them around with us. If we don't know the problems, we can't pray.

For Our Finances

Another area for trusting God is our finances. Economizing and investing in our future when we are young blesses our children when we are old. If husbandry of our resources now means we won't require subsidizing later, it's worth the sacrifices. Financial circumstances aren't always in our control. Circumstances change, reverses take place, but a thoughtful saving and investment program under the direction of a Christian counselor can help us do our part. Sometimes our finances require discussion, but constant worry doesn't exhibit faith. Use our resources wisely. Then trust God to provide for our needs as He promised. Concentrate on making deposits in heaven's bank. "But store up for yourselves treasures in heaven, where moth and rust do not destroy, and where thieves do not break in and steal" (Matthew 6:20).

In today's society, it's common for old people to fear violence, robbery, mugging—not unfounded fears. Fear creates negative conversations, however. Take sensible steps for protection and don't allow anxieties to dominate our conversation or to cheat us of enjoying life. Pray this scripture: "Do not cast me away when I am old; do not forsake me when my strength is gone" (Psalm 71:9). Exaggerated fears cause us to make decisions that narrow our experiences. Dwell on what's good in society, not what's negative, when talking to the younger generation. They know the problems, but find their repetition unpleasant.

For Our Health

"He will renew your life and sustain you in your old age" (Ruth 4:15a). We can reduce the concerns of our children if we follow healthy living patterns. Eat well, exercise, follow our doctor's directions. It's amazing how many old people spend good money on a doctor visit and then ignore his instructions. Get the glasses we need, a hearing aid if necessary. Use all the resources God supplies through His people to function at the top level possible. Find ways to fill our days rather than requiring others to fill them for us. By tending to our health where it's within our power, we reduce the burden we are to our children.

Accept Guidance from the Children

When we grow old, if our children have learned responsibility, it's natural for them to begin to change their role in our lives. Where we used to protect them, care for them, guide them, and advise them, now they are doing those things for us. If we can accept this reversal as natural and an outgrowth of love for us, we can cooperate instead of buck them. Cooperating doesn't mean we hand over all our decisions to them. It means we won't resent their concerns and ignore their input. Watching us make sensible housing arrangements, take steps to ensure our safety and health, find solutions to problems, and exhibit contentment will ease our children's minds.

Housing Arrangements

Everyone is different, but the results of my survey indicated living in the same house with our children was usually unsatisfactory. Both the younger and the older generation expressed rancor with this arrangement. To prevent irritations from mounting, some distance is beneficial. As the older generation, we can determine to supply the emotional and physical distance to the best of our ability, even if we are living under the same roof.

By planning for old age when we are young, we can hope to finance a good living situation. By putting the happiness of our children as our first consideration and placing what sounds pleasant to us as second place, we hope to find an arrangement that enhances their love for us and doesn't damage the respect and tenderness of our relationship. "Nobody should seek his own good, but the good of others" (1 Corinthians 10:24). If the parents knew of the loss of patience and respect some of the younger generation expressed to me after living too close, they would wish they had chosen another solution.

Leaning too heavily for support on one child over others sometimes fosters resentment between the children. After we are gone, we want loving relationships between our children.

Our Possessions

Sort and organize our belongings to spare our children some of the pain when we die. Otherwise, in their need to finish the work, interesting or valuable items may get tossed. By giving some of our items as an inheritance while we are living, we can see them enjoy our things. Detach ourselves emotionally from our belongings. They are trivial when we look at life from the perspective of eternity. We can't require our children to attach importance to our possessions. Ella labeled the bottom of treasured family objects with a strip of tape giving the name of the original owner and any other interesting tidbits. One bowl's label revealed it was purchased at the first world's fair. The children, not knowing, would have pitched it. Instead they treasure it.

Phil was a pack rat. Over the years he stuffed box after box full of grocery receipts, junk mail, advertisements—and important documents. Every box required sorting. His sons never knew when they would turn up an insurance policy or a letter full of family history among the piles of junk. Their patience with the tedious procedure was renewed when they unearthed a diamond ring from one box. Have mercy on your kids—organize, eliminate, and label.

Driving Ability

✧ **Ted and Sharon** ✧

"Stop! The light is red," Sharon said. Ted applied the brakes.

"What's that?" Max, Ted's older brother asked from the back seat. "Do you want to stop buying Lysol that's red?"

"No, I said the stop light's red," Sharon shouted to her deaf brother-in-law. "The light's green now, Ted," Sharon told him. Ted started up.

"Is there a blight on the cream?" Deaf Max tried to follow the conversation.

Sharon ignored him. "Turn here, Ted. Can you see the arrow pointing into the grocery parking lot?"

"What arrow?" Ted asked. "Where's the turn off?"

"About 7 yards ahead. Slow now, a little farther, a little more, there, turn now, right here. Watch that car!" Sharon screamed.

"Close call." Even Max could hear Sharon's shout.

"That's it," Sharon declared as they safely eased into a parking place in front of the grocery store. "We're taking a taxi from now on to get groceries. Maybe we need to make other arrangements." Between Ted peering at the shelves from an inch away trying to see what is what and shouting at Max for the next item on the list, we look like a comedy team, thought Sharon.

Our ability to drive is a central factor in what living

arrangements are best for us as we age. Our children will have peace of mind if we stop driving before we become a hazard. Sometimes we need to stop driving before the state licensing department recognizes the fact.

Important Contributions for Our Old Age

Intercession

Don't waste time and energy regretting our declining abilities. We may well perform the most important role of our entire lives when we pray for our families and friends in our old age. The impact of our prayers may change society and lives for generations to come. When we can no longer do what we used to do, we gain extra time for prayer. By praying, we are providing a contribution beyond what we'll comprehend in this life.

Family History

Write it down; speak it into a tape recorder. Talk about it—but not over and over endlessly. One great-grandmother kept a notebook for each of her great-grandchildren. In it she recorded memories of her life, of her children's childhood, and of her children's children. She saved a few pictures and cards that each person had sent to her and included those along with her own miscellaneous doodles. The stuffed notebooks became irreplaceable treasures of family history and love.

Love

When we do not bear the responsibility for raising

the little people in our family, we can offer love and acceptance that is not tinged by the need to also administer discipline. Love unconditionally, warts and all. Sometimes advice travels better when it skips a generation. As the oldest generation in the family, we may find the opportunity to suggest and transmit philosophy beyond what our children can do for their own children.

With God's help Psalm 92:14 can describe us when we are old. "They will still bear fruit in old age, they will stay fresh and green." With God's help we can continue to bless our family in our old age. Advance planning will minimize worrying our children.

- ✧ Plan ahead for old age.
- ✧ Develop a thankful spirit.
- ✧ Stay flexible in our thinking.
- ✧ Develop listening skills.
- ✧ Practice consideration for others.
- ✧ Grow in trusting God.
- ✧ Be responsible about our finances and health.
- ✧ Accept guidance from the children.
- ✧ Make considerate housing arrangements.
- ✧ Organize our belongings.
- ✧ Don't drive when no longer safe.
- ✧ Contribute prayer, a sense of heritage, and love.

Appendix 1

Ten Do's and Don'ts for Mothers-in-Law

With God as our source for wisdom, understanding, healthy expectations, and beneficial attitudes, we can enjoy our grown children and their spouses. Regardless of past problems and failures, God gives us a new tomorrow full of hope for His goodness to our family. With God's help we can concentrate on the do's in this list, minimize the don'ts in our lives and thank Him for every happy moment with our family.

✧ 1 ✧

Don't become discouraged with your performance as a mother-in-law.
Do trust God to help you be a blessing to your family.

✧ 2 ✧

Don't harbor in-law resentments.
Do forgive and forget.

✧ 3 ✧

Don't rehash negative incidents in your mind.
Do concentrate on the in-law's good traits.

✧ 4 ✧

Don't be careless about your relationships.

Do believe God cares about and helps with family relationships.

✧ 5 ✧

Don't try to muddle along in your own strength.
Do develop a regular prayer and Bible-reading pattern.

✧ 6 ✧

Don't ignore hurt feelings.
Do apologize quickly when your in-law is offended.

✧ 7 ✧

Don't expect too much from your in-laws.
Do relax and enjoy your family.

✧ 8 ✧

Don't take it for granted your love shows.
Do find creative ways to convey love.

✧ 9 ✧

Don't waste time regretting failures.
Do forgive yourself and find ways to improve relationships.

✧ 10 ✧

Don't be afraid of your role.
Do believe God to make you a good mother-in-law.

Appendix 2

The Engagement and Wedding

✧ Gretchen ✧

"Can't we start without her? The rehearsal was supposed to begin an hour ago," Gretchen fumed, pulling her bridegroom, George, away from the milling bridesmaids and groomsmen.

"I guess it's okay to start without my mom," George said. "Something must have held her up after the rehearsal dinner at the restaurant."

"That's her own fault," Gretchen bristled. "Without so much as a word to me, she re-scheduled the rehearsal dinner to before the rehearsal. I knew after the rehearsal was better. Is this the kind of consideration I can expect from your mom?"

✧ June and Marcia ✧

"We found a charming little club near the church for Marcia and Guy to have a lovely sit-down wedding reception." Guy's mother, June, smiled at Marcia's mother, Hilda.

"You found what?" Hilda glanced quickly at her daughter.

"Guy's family always has fancy, sit-down dinners for their wedding receptions," Marcia nervously explained. She turned to her future mother-in-law. "Mom and I hadn't planned on a sit-down dinner."

"The club's more attractive than your church hall. It's the ideal place for a reception," June gushed.

"Well, June, if you and Guy want to finance the 'ideal' place, we might consider it." Frost iced Hilda's voice.

"Oh, no, it's the bride's place to pay for the wedding."

"In that case, my family always has our receptions in the church hall," Hilda said.

"But the club's more elegant," June pressed her opinion. "Weddings are elegant occasions."

Later Marcia told me, "I should have known right then I was going to have problems with my mother-in-law."

What You Can Do Ahead of the Wedding

"If it is possible, as far as it depends on you, live at peace with everyone" (Romans 12:18). Before the wedding prepare for successful relationships. If your child is already married, don't despair. Most of these suggestions work at any stage.

Avoid Wedding Plan Clashes

"Let us therefore make every effort to do what leads to peace and to mutual edification" (Romans 14:19). Quarrels and wrangling over wedding plans dampen a good beginning for in-law relationships.

Classic wisdom advises the groom's mother to wear beige and keep her mouth shut. Safe, but let's go beyond neutral to foster good relationships. Wedding planning supplies opportunities to create good will. It's a good idea for the mother of the bride to include the groom's mother by asking her wishes on a few of the wedding details. While the wedding must satisfy the bride's heart and fit her or her parent's pocketbook, incorporating some of the desires of the groom's family is possible without blowing the budget or drastically changing wedding plans.

The groom's mother, for her part, can offer to help the bride. Volunteer to run errands, prepare reception food, or decorate the reception hall. Help is usually welcome if it doesn't mean altering plans. Trust the Lord to mold the plans. The details of the wedding loom large at the moment, but are dwarfed by the significance of a lifetime relationship. They are not worth risking ill-will.

Cultivate Friendship Ahead of the Wedding

"A man that hath friends must shew himself friendly" (Proverbs 18:24a, KJV). Mothers-in-law profit from showing friendship. Small gifts and friendly notes filled with appreciation boost friendship before the wedding. I still remember my happy glow of acceptance when my future mother-in-law in Virginia sent a welcoming letter to me in Indiana enclosing a pretty handkerchief. Gold would not have pleased me more. I still have that welcoming gift.

Chat on the phone. Plan a fun activity together. Strive to make the fiancée feel like one of the family. Searching out the young person's opinion helps disarm caution and convey acceptance.

Guard Our Conversation

"Set a guard over my mouth, O LORD; keep watch

over the door of my lips" (Psalm 141:3). Once our child's emotional attachment switches to his or her future mate as we mentioned in chapter 3, expect our child to later repeat whatever we say when the girl or boyfriend is absent. Some children use wisdom culling our conversation to leave out antagonizing comments. We'd better not count on such wisdom and guard against hasty remarks. Long before the wedding day we need to set a watch on our tongues.

A Special Evening for Sharing

Initiating an evening with the engaged couple to talk about marriage philosophy before the wedding prevents future misunderstandings. Before they begin making decisions as a married couple, the kids are not defensive but eager to learn. All young couples want to escape the pitfalls of marital disharmony. They want our approval. Talking about our philosophy before marriage doesn't convey disapproval of their mistakes or decisions because they haven't made any yet to condemn. We can speak our thoughts without seeming to judge them. This special evening helps the young couple understand our intentions and forestalls wrong interpretations.

One girl told me she appreciated her mother-in-law because she knew, no matter what the woman did, she meant well. The purpose of this prenuptial talk is to establish that we mean well.

If early in the dating relationship, parents opposed the child dating this particular person or pointed out failings in the potential mate, then this prenuptial talk is perfect for overcoming negative feelings. Load this special time with acceptance and approval.

How to Have a Special Evening

With three of our children, my husband and I arranged a dinner evening with the engaged couple explaining how we desired to relate to them as married adults. For the fourth couple, it was breakfast in a private corner of a restaurant. A private and a relaxed atmosphere stimulates openness and lessens nervousness. Explain the purpose, to talk about how we view our role as in-laws. Learning of our best intentions, we hope the couple will have compassion when we fail. At least they will know the offending behavior is because of our imperfect nature, not our philosophy.

Every family will have its own ideas of what's important. Boil the list of items down to the essentials. If we present numerous areas of cardinal importance, the children will leave the conference feeling hopeless about their abilities to live up to our expectations. Worse, they might leave with hostile feelings because they sense demands. We want them to believe we are comfortable and supportive of their new family unit. We want to increase our understanding of each other, not cause greater misunderstanding.

Suggested Topics

The pre-marriage conference offers the safest time to say what we consider important ingredients in home life. After marriage the couple will think such discussions imply disapproval of their home life. The following topics were ones we used in our own family.

Stay-at-Home Mothers

Do you hope your grandchildren's mother will stay home with preschoolers? Now is the safest time to say babies benefit from having mother at home. Suggest that the couple make major purchases and financial decisions based only on one income. Then, in the event of an unplanned pregnancy, they will have the financial freedom to make an unemotional decision. Make sure the couple knows these are only opinions. The newlyweds must recognize you give them the right to make their own decisions as circumstances change.

Daily Devotions

"I love those who love me, and those who seek me find me" (Proverbs 8:17). Do you believe daily devotions for the family are important? This evening provides a non-lecturing atmosphere to say prayer and Bible reading are the undergirding pillars of a healthy home. Since the two haven't failed to have quiet time as a married couple yet, it is good advice, not a condemning intrusion. After the wedding, urging Bible time creates resentment.

He Is All Yours

✧ *Theresa and Sarah Jean* ✧

"My baby. I'm going to miss my son so much. I can't bear for you to move very far away," Theresa's future mother-in-law, Sarah Jean, moaned again and again before the wedding.

Actually, when her son married, Sarah Jean let him go successfully, but Theresa never gave her credit for it. Theresa's antenna was up, searching for signs of the attitude that had distressed her earlier. She filled my questionnaire with bitter comments about her "clinging" mother-in-law.

Verbalize the intention to release our child into the tender keeping of his intended. If it is a son marrying, the bride wonders how his mother pictures her place in the marriage. The girl is tickled to land the guy, and ready to jealously defend her position, not only from young rivals but from any rivalry she sees or imagines with Mom. Time makes her more secure; but, meanwhile, declare him free. Telling the bride we recognize the changes marriage makes in our ties to our son, removes us as a threat and prevents her from misinterpreting us as clinging. Be sure to read chapters 2 and 3 for more on this topic.

Promise to Speak Well of One Another

Titus 3:2 says to slander no one. A family pledge to apply the verse to our in-laws creates a trusting family atmosphere. Promise not to discuss the shortcomings of one in-law with another in-law or with your own children, then keep the promise. Extract a promise for the same treatment in return. When people hear someone criticized, they fear they receive the same treatment when they are absent. One lady wrote, "If the bird tweets in my yard, it will tweet some more when it returns home." Mutual grace for one another's shortcomings improves relationships. Since in-laws readily spot our flaws, we might as well ask for their grace ahead of time. Knowing we recognize our imperfections enlists their desire to overlook our failings.

"When they measure themselves by themselves and compare themselves with themselves, they are not wise" (2 Corinthians 10:12b). Diversity of talents and interests creates family strength. Rejoice in everyone's strength and cover their weaknesses. Make a prenuptial pact to not make comparisons between family members. Pledge not to compare in-law's personality traits, flaws or talents with each other.

Express hope for friendship to flourish between all the siblings and their spouses.

Give Them Space

We said, "We don't know how many phone calls are too many or even when they're convenient, so for this first year, we plan to leave the phoning up to you, unless we have important information or arrangements to make." To keep this promise we smacked each others hands as we reached for the phone and laughed over our excuses for wanting to call.

The same concept applied to visits. Not knowing how much contact the couple needed, we told them to initiate the visiting in the early months of their marriage. We did not want them to feel neglected, but neither did we want to be a nuisance. After the critical first year, we better understood their lifestyles, and we were freer in our calls and visits.

We explained that we like to gather the whole family together whenever we have out-of-town relatives visiting, but we would understand if the couples couldn't come. At least they knew what mattered to us. As it turned out, they indulge us with lots of get togethers.

Christmas and Other Red Letter Days

While we naturally desire to spend important holidays with our complete family gathered around us, we must recognize that now we must share our loved ones. We should be flexible and not demanding. Some couples feel compelled to spend each holiday shuttling back and forth between their families.

Think and talk about the possiblity of beginning a new extended family tradition by gathering together on a day other than what you might normally have done. Again, find out what the couple wishes. At this point, they may not know. Be willing to let them experiment. Express our desire to see them as often as they spend holidays with the other side, but don't take offense if we don't see them for the particular day that we desire.

A System for Airing Grievances
✧ Sally and Billie Jo ✧

Sally, twenty years old when she married, knew it all. Apparently, she considered her mission to remake her mother-in-law, Billie Jo. Often the mail brought Billie Jo letters laced with phrases like, "I am upset because you should not have . . ." or, "Why didn't you . . ." Regularly the phone rang for more correction of her omissions or commissions. All Billie Jo's ways were subject to comment.

Although exasperated, Billie Jo tried to meet each occasion with the grace she wished her daughter-in-law would extend to her. After a few years of accommodating the girl's demands and holding her tongue, Sally became more and more accepting until now the relationship jogs along well.

If our child's mate is irritated with some of our actions or words, how can they let us know? Since our child knows us better and is more comfortable with us, we suggested he tell us when we strain the relationship. Because we aren't mind-readers, we need to be told if we are damaging our relationship. Otherwise we endlessly repeat our mistakes. As difficult as it is to confront our failings, facing them is better than risking a cool relationship by digging a deep hole of resentment. Granting the privilege of correcting us helps motivate us to examine our actions rather than risk confrontation. However, only give permission for the major annoyances. Sally wanted to correct every trivial interaction. We don't need to ask our in-laws to re-make us.

By offering friendship ahead of the wedding, cooperating with wedding plans and establishing our best intentions during a special evening before the wedding, we can help begin our relationship with the new in-law on a good foundation.

- ✧ Avoid disagreement over wedding plans.
- ✧ Cultivate friendship before the wedding.
- ✧ Guard our conversation.
- ✧ Plan a special evening to communicate our attitudes.
- ✧ Pledge to speak well of one another.
- ✧ Pledge not to make comparisons.
- ✧ Pledge not to monopolize their time.
- ✧ Discuss holidays.
- ✧ Discuss a method for handling problems.